TAKE
THE REINS!

7 Secrets to Inspired Leadership

SHARI JAEGER GOODWIN

Printed in the United States of America.

ISBN: 978-0-9891844-0-3

Jaeger2, LLC
P.O. Box 493
Marshall, VA 20116
540-364-9505
www.jaeger2.com

Limits of Liability and Disclaimer of Warranty

The author and publisher shall not be liable for your misuse of this material. This book is strictly for informational and educational purposes.

Warning—Disclaimer

The purpose of this book is to educate and entertain. The author and/or publisher do not guarantee that anyone following these techniques, suggestions, tips, ideas, or strategies will become successful. The author and/or publisher shall have neither liability nor responsibility to anyone with respect to any loss or damage caused, or alleged to be caused, directly or indirectly by the information contained in this book. Further, readers should be aware that internet websites listed in this work may have changed or disappeared between when this work was written and when it is read.

Acknowledgments

I am so grateful to all of the people who have shared in my journey.

To my husband who loves me unconditionally and patiently scrutinized each word of the manuscript.

To my dad who inspired and encouraged my writing gene and to my mom for believing that anything is possible. And to both for their steadfast support.

To my sister for her love and trust throughout my entire life.

To my brother for his direct and astute eye and great sense of humor (and for coming up with the title, way cool!).

To my uncles for their creative genius and willingness to believe. And to my extended family for their humor, brilliance, and deep connections.

To my friends who love animals and appreciate the awesome wisdom of the natural world.

To my corporate colleagues who gave me opportunities to learn, grow, give back, and be part of an outstanding team.

To the "dog pack" of my youth and all of my animal friends.

To my clients for taking a chance and stepping into their greatness no matter how scary.

To my book coach who helped make my book dream a reality.

To my horses, Dixie, Frescoe, Cali, Lila, and Noble for teaching me difficult and beautiful lessons about life and for always keeping me humble and grounded.

You have all impacted my life in profound ways. I am eternally grateful.

Contents

Introduction

I bridge two worlds. I help leaders build and lead profitable businesses that they love. By way of the horse.

What?

It's true.

My areas of focus include strategy, relationship-building, and goal achievement. I help others empower the "other 90 percent" of their potential to optimize results. My medium is the horse. The results? Fantastic and quantifiable.

Several clients have doubled their revenue, one had her best financial year ever, another secured a dream job as a chief executive officer, and others have developed exciting new brands through our work together. And many have experienced huge positive transformation beyond the business realm into their mindsets, relationships, and daily lives.

I wrote this book to share these leadership "secrets" learned from horses and to give you a look inside this powerful learning modality from my own experiences and those of my clients. For privacy, all names have been changed, but the stories are real.

Each "secret" addresses factors critical to success at work and life, and gives you tips for using them in your own world.

This book answers the question: How do you inspire and motivate others to follow your lead?

The "secrets" found within will help you find your authentic power to gain the trust of others, overcome overwhelm, conquer fear, and accomplish great things. And whether it's to lead staff, lead a client, lead a prospect through your sales process, or lead yourself, the fundamental skills presented in this book will help get you where you want to go. I know this for sure.

I know this because I've lived it. Every part. The fear and excitement of tackling multi-million-dollar proposals, the overwhelm of entrepreneurship, the dogged pursuit of new clients. The trust of a great staff. And the pain of a not-so-great staff.

My latest jump off the corporate track began several years ago.

I was working as a director at a prestigious corporation. And although I told myself I was happy, I felt unsettled. Restless. I had lots of evidence of "success" from years of hard work—a great job, a wonderful husband, a beautiful property, horses, and dogs. But, I knew I could do more. I craved deeper meaning and connection in my work and to make an impact in the lives of others.

I felt urged to blend my business expertise with my other passion: working with horses. I had learned so much from horses. And many of those lessons were central to my success in business. Working with horses for over 25 years had given me skills in leadership, sales, and negotiation that I had been applying to my corporate job and with other business clients for years.

From horses, I learned to use the "other 90 percent" of my potential—energy, intention, and nonverbal communication—to influence desired outcomes. But no one knew. It was my little secret, and it was hugely powerful.

For example, in each position throughout my career, I had been quickly promoted to a leadership role by using the skills learned from horses. My supervisors asked me to work with some of the most difficult clients and lead the most demanding projects. I eagerly agreed, always ready for a new challenge. I directed multi-million-dollar projects, led winning proposal efforts, and supervised numerous staff. And my clients were thrilled with the results.

I also used these skills to take an information technology startup from $0 to $2.1 million in its first year. And the staff included just me and one other person. When I cold-called prospective clients, they seemed a bit baffled by my style and said, "You know, you don't seem like a salesperson. And you don't seem to be reading from a script."

Probably because I wasn't really selling (I was just having a conversation) and I didn't have a script. My closing rates were super high.

But blending the business world with my horsemanship skills? This seemed a bit weird and unconventional, even to me.

In the horse world, leadership is key. Under the right human leadership, the most shy and insecure horse can blossom into a brilliant, confident performer. So can explosive, athletic, opinionated types. I believe the same is true for humans in the workforce.

It's all about inspiring strengths and giving these strengths focus, direction, and a vehicle for full expression and complete engagement. An engaged workforce usually sticks around. And we all know that high staff retention is crucial to profit generation.

But it starts with the leader. Staff performance reflects the confidence of the leader. And the success of a small business reflects the confidence of its owner.

So, after a few years of toying with how I could blend my worlds into a focused service, the pull was too strong to deny any longer. The skills learned from horses needed to be shared with the business world, no matter how weird.

I developed my own leadership model based on my experiences in both worlds and created *Alpha Horse Leadership Training for HUMANS*™. And then I resigned. I jumped off the corporate track to start my firm.

I left a six-figure job that I loved in the middle of a recession. Yes, I did. The timing was bad. The country was in a terrible economic state and thousands of people were losing their jobs. But my desire was unyielding.

Why did I take this risk? Because I am driven by the question "How can I add the most value to the world?" And although I knew that I was adding value in that corporate job, I also knew that I could make a bigger impact and help more people if I made a change.

And here's the truth: I wasn't even entirely sure what this would look like. But I jumped anyway.

Was I scared? You bet. I had worked at that firm for nine years. I served as director of program strategy for the large global engineering firm and had earned autonomy and respect. Previously, I worked as a management consultant, an environmental scientist for 20 years, a technical staffing specialist, and a horse trainer and breeder.

Now I walk a solitary path, forging new territory, and at times it's rather scary. My work requires that I push aside all of my insecurities, be seen, and be fully present for my clients. No matter what. I must walk my talk. And I am tested on it daily by those who can see right through a false face. My herd of horses.

From my life experience, I know three things for sure:

- You can create something out of "nothing."

- You can make money doing what you love.

- At any point, you can reinvent yourself.

I know these things because I have done them over and over as I strive to fulfill my own potential and lead a joyous life of my own design. A life in which the fear of failure is dimmed by the radiant possibilities beyond the risks. A life that blends my passions, skills, and experience in a way that keeps me fully engaged and challenged. And inspires others to live their own unique greatness.

I invite you to look around your world. Your world is a reflection of you. Your beliefs, your confidence, your choices, your trust, your goals. Are you the leader of your own life? Do you live by your own design? Do you inspire and motivate others? Are you happy? Are you sure?

If not, no worries. You can always reinvent yourself. Sometimes it just takes a small tweak in your perspective. Reflect on what you need. What you want. And give it to yourself. Life is too short to be put on hold. Live it now!

Finally, this book is my contribution to the growing body of literature on optimizing our potential and relationship-building, areas I remain committed to in my own life and continue to explore each day.

I hope you enjoy these "secrets" and I look forward to hearing about how the lessons learned from the herd help you step into your place of power as an inspired leader.

And be sure to check out my leadership model for photos of the horses in action (see www.jaeger2.com). This model is great for relationship-building for executives, business owners, and salespersons. It also works well for organizational development and writing sales copy. And you don't need a horse to implement it!

Here's to living your greatness!

Shari Jaeger Goodwin

Chapter 1

Early Lessons

I'm lucky. I love what I do and it feels natural. Now. But it wasn't always this way. It took a lot of bumps and bruises to learn the secrets to inspired leadership. The first lessons were pretty rough. Here I'll share some of those lessons, give you a peak at my non-human teachers, and introduce you to my horses, the instructors at *Alpha Horse Leadership Training for HUMANS*™.

Let's start with a look at ego. Ah, yes.

Early on, my ego would get the best of me and I'd end up frustrated with the horse and sometimes feeling like a loser. I would go to the stable with a specific agenda and plan (e.g., to jump a course of fences), but my horse Dixie, a fiery chestnut mare, would have other things on her mind. Like spooking at bushes, whinnying wildly at horses in the field, and making nasty faces at other horses in the ring. Anything to avoid taking direction from me.

Although I had the right "gadgets," the right bit, saddle, a variety of training approaches, and took lessons from a trainer, Dixie didn't believe that I was worthy of her attention. That I was a safe place. Someone she could trust with her life. And I wasn't. Yet.

Dixie was an alpha mare—the lead mare in her herd—and also a young, high-energy ex-racehorse. Although I had good intentions, she made me nervous and my anxious energy triggered frustrating behavior. Her flight instincts were top form. In her eyes, I was weak, unworthy of her trust, time, or attention. She was right. And it hurt. But I loved her deeply.

In my 20s, I'd stagger into the office of my corporate job Monday mornings after a weekend spent riding. My back and neck stiff and sore from slamming into the ground off my horse. "How was your weekend?" my co-workers would ask. "Fantastic," I'd reply, a big smile across my face as I limped down the hall. I was determined to make this relationship work.

So I kept at it. I worked with Dixie and as many horses as I could to better understand their unique preferences, raise my own abilities, and build relationships based on trust and understanding.

Thankfully, I became more self-aware. I learned from my failures and began to use my entire being to influence the horse. My energy. Where I focused my attention. How I held my body. The timing and intensity of my request. My intention and commitment to a task. Even my breath.

I learned to recognize and resolve my anxiety through breathing, consciously releasing tension and visualizing positive outcomes. I made adjustments to address what was happening *now*, consider options, and let go of the agenda I had planned for the session. And I found that when I was relaxed and intentional, I could see what the horse needed from me as a leader. I could "hear" its questions and "feel" its emotions. My newfound empathy and confidence allowed me to adjust my own energy and emotional state, then offer the horse an option best suited to its needs. When I directed the horse this way, it usually happily obliged.

This new approach centered on empathy—the capacity to experience the emotions of another—and my own self-awareness changed everything. This was a turning point in my horsemanship and had huge influences on my professional life outside of horses. It wasn't all about me, how I felt, what I wanted, what I knew, or even what someone else told me to do. For best results, I needed to truly understand what the "other" desired and needed. And in this case, the "other" was a horse.

My reward for learning these lessons? I developed a strong bond with Dixie and we won many competitions. Bystanders watching us compete during cross-country jumping would comment, "Wow, she looks so happy and relaxed." And she was. I also gained a small reputation as the person to see if you had a difficult horse. Mares mostly. Mares with strong opinions that just didn't seem to want to do what their owners desired. Horses that scared their people. Horses that reflected the confusion and fear in their people. And I worked with many riders who just wanted to develop deeper relationships with their horse.

I also incorporated these teachings in my business relationships. I learned how to inspire the "other" to share what they really wanted. The "others" included my boss, my co-workers, my staff, my clients, and others involved in our projects. I gained their confidence and created a safe emotional space for them to share their thoughts and desires with me. To be heard fully. To thoroughly discuss project requirements, options, timelines, budgets, and challenges as partners on the same team.

I did this by using energy, intention and nonverbal communication learned from the horses. I consciously shifted my own energy, intention, and body language throughout meetings to offer a continual vibration of neutrality and possibility. An energy of openness. This energy is nonthreatening and safe. Your body is relaxed, your breathing is steady, your eyes are curious and soft. This energy allows all to be heard unjudged and builds trust. This was pivotal to my success as a leader both in my corporate life and as a business owner. With trust, you can do anything.

I also learned that there is always more to learn. Just when you think you've learned something fully, another horse, person, or situation will come along to challenge your views. I am a lifelong student and learn something new every day.

But the horses were not my only teachers of nonverbal communication, energy, and self-awareness. Before the horses were the dogs.

But First, Dogs!

From as far back as I can remember, I've loved nature and dogs and horses and considered myself a student of animal behavior and communication.

As a 9-year old, I assembled a pack of neighborhood dogs every morning before school just to watch them play and interact, or choose not to engage at all. This was well before leash laws and dog park days; all the dogs were free to roam wherever they pleased.

My morning dog pack ritual lasted three years and I became known by adults in the area as "the dog girl." In fact, a local artist wrote a poem about me. Some people even dropped off stray dogs on our front porch, much to the displeasure of my mother.

I loved getting to know the unique personalities of each dog. Some were shy, others playful, some dominant, others submissive. I loved to watch them roll around on the ground, grab each other's ears and necks then leap in the air and race around in happy circles. It was also clear when one had violated some code of "dogdom." A growl and sharp snap would be followed immediately by the offender's silent submission often while upside down on his back. Forgiveness was equally fast and the pack would quickly resume playing and sniffing around. In those days, my jeans pockets were filled with dog treats, the leftover crumbles forming a goo after going through the wash.

The pack taught me early lessons in effective leadership, living in the "now," and the importance of forgive and forget.

In eighth grade, I was hired by a local boarding kennel that catered to dogs and cats. My job was to feed the animals, clean the runs, and often help the resident groomer with shampooing. I stayed in this position through my senior year of high school, promoted to kennel manager after the first three years.

I frequently worked alone on weekends and holidays when the kennel was closed and formed close relationships with the dogs and cats. I administered medication, created special dishes for picky eaters, and cleaned the runs until my fingers cracked from the bleach. I also consoled the stressed-out animals who struggled in this foreign environment. I sat quietly outside the runs of dogs hiding in the corner refusing to eat and too afraid to move. Eventually, I was usually able to get even the most frightened animal to engage and relax. Here I learned more lessons on the subtleties of energy, the power of eye contact and body position, comfort zone, and, most importantly, when to back off.

These early lessons in nonverbal communication remain with me and I'm forever grateful.

But now, it's mostly about horses. So let's meet the herd!

Meet the Horses!

Here is a brief introduction to the members of my herd, the most important contributors to this work. All have unique talents and skills and continue to influence me daily. Each plays a role in my signature program, *Alpha Horse Leadership Training for HUMANS*™. They keep me learning and humble, and always have some new challenge for me. I am thankful for their gifts.

Dixie

Dixie is my first horse and an entire book could be written about our time together. She's a hot-headed chestnut Thoroughbred mare and we have a tremendous partnership spanning 25 years (and counting!). Dixie challenged my leadership in ways that I never thought I would survive, yet we persevered and built a steadfast relationship based on trust, commitment, and a desire for excellence. We competed in dressage, jumping, and combined training, and she was a superstar. After parting ways for her retirement, she came back into my life a few years ago and I'm grateful to be with her for the rest of time. She's now 28. Her heart is unsurpassed and her power is everlasting. I share her teachings in every part of my life.

Cali

Cali, also known as Candlelight (her registered name), is a classy grey Oldenburg mare from Germany. She is also registered with the American Hanoverian Society. When we met, she was 4 years old and had just started her riding training. I loved her immediately, and her lofty gaits and regal presence placed us high in the ribbons at local dressage shows, often in first place. However, as we progressed in our training, she decided that she was tired of the riding ring. We switched to jumping and although she was an incredibly powerful jumper, it was a bit scary for me when she flung her body as high as she could over a jump just for fun. So, since our favorite activity together was trail riding, we spent many hours walking quietly together in nature. Then she found her real calling: inspiring and motivating others to find their truth and walk in their authentic power. Cali is an absolute master at this work and has been deemed "the Cali Lama" by her fans since she's so Zen. As of the writing of this book, we have been together for 13 years.

Lila

Lila was bred on our farm and is our first foal. Her dam was a Thoroughbred ex-racehorse who won 10 races and her sire was an Elite Hanoverian stallion, Wallstreet Kid. Lila was a spunky little sweetheart from the moment she was born. She's an athletic, dramatic redhead with a heart of gold. We sold her as a 3-year-old to a wonderful owner who took Lila to college. A series of financial and personal struggles prompted her owner to sell Lila several years later. I hastily bought her back and we competed in dressage for a couple of years. When she was focused and relaxed, she was perfect. However, she was also prone to leaping about when frightened. But once the drama passed, she was calm and sweet again; she kept me on my toes! Lila had to be retired from riding at an early age due to a strange neurologic condition. It was initially pretty devastating for us both since she loves to work, but then we created our equine-assisted coaching practice and she is just brilliant. She is patient and kind, and loves to help people discover their inner leaders. I am thrilled to have her back in my life.

Noble

Noble is Lila's little brother. Three years younger, he shares the same dam and the sires were half-brothers. His sire is the Elite Hanoverian stallion, Winterprinz. Noble was bred on our farm and has been with me since he was born. Another fancy chestnut, he is super smart, athletic, opinionated, and sensitive, and loves to show off. We've trained lightly in dressage but have never competed due to one thing or another. We love to play at liberty free in the arena, ride without a bit, and do exercises telepathically. He's a fantastic teacher of leadership in our equine-assisted coaching practice and keeps the energy level high. There's never a dull moment with this guy!

Frescoe

Frescoe is my first foal, my first gelding, my first warmblood, and my first bay horse. Prior to Frescoe, I had owned only chestnut mares! We've been together since he was born 14 years ago. His mother was a Thoroughbred and his sire is a Belgium Warmblood, Nevada. Frescoe is brave, sweet, gorgeous, and hugely intelligent. We used to call him "the little professor" when he was a foal since he observed the world with curiosity and deep intrigue. He is my main riding partner and has the perfect blend of focus and play. He has an impressive work ethic and supports the group work in our coaching practice.

Now let's take a look at why horses make such perfect partners for teaching inspired leadership.

Chapter 2

Awareness and Horses

As you saw in Chapter 1, most of my early lessons from horses centered on gaining self-awareness. And on better understanding the unique needs of the horse.

Self-awareness and awareness of another's emotions are key elements of emotional intelligence, a skill vital to inspired leadership. The term "emotional intelligence" has been around since the 1960s, but gained broad acclaim in 1998 with the publication of Daniel Goleman's famous book *Working with Emotional Intelligence*. Emotional intelligence is the ability to identify, assess, and manage your emotions and to recognize and influence the emotional state of others.

All experts agree that people in the workforce with high emotional intelligence advance faster than those who lack this skill. Inspired leaders excel in this area.

So, why is this important?

Because as a leader, your job is to get results—to achieve goals. You must be clear and direct to keep your team motivated and on track. Both you and your team are affected by your emotional energy. Fear-based emotions like anxiety and mistrust breed stress and insecurity, and impact your ability to get things done. You waste time and money thrashing about in confusion. Your team struggles to keep up. And you may not know why.

But the fix could be simple. Just a shift to a more calm emotional state allows you to see clearly, consider options, and lead from a place of power. The faster you can do this, the quicker you can re-establish trust and get the results you desire.

And horses can help you.

How?

There are three ways: 1) The horse is a master at reading intention, 2) the horse is concerned only with the present moment—the now, and 3) the horse validates congruence—the energetic state where what you think, feel, say, and do, align.

To see your true self is a gift. Although sometimes you may not like what you see. Honest feedback can be painful, validating, and also empowering.

There is no better way to get honest feedback than by interacting with a horse. Horses are completely objective and hold no judgment. They read your emotional state and true intention, and show you this truth from moment to moment. But be warned. Seeing your truth can be quite humbling. It is not always what you think.

Throughout this book, I will share examples from real experiences that show you how horses are helping others optimize their potential and be great leaders. Each "secret" is supported by stories from my workshops and private sessions. I also offer some of my personal experiences.

In this chapter, we'll explore how horses teach emotional intelligence by reading intention, living in the now, and validating congruence. And, I'll give you a behind-the-scenes look at what happens in my "office," during equine assisted coaching sessions. Let's dive in!

The Horse Is a Master at Reading Intention

As prey animals in the wild, a horse's survival is based on its accurate assessment of another's intention: an answer to the question "Is this a threat or not?" If a horse misreads the intention of a predator, the consequence could be its death. Even domesticated horses show a strong fight-or-flight response and run from a threat unless trapped. If the horse cannot flee, it fights—rearing up, striking out with its front legs, biting, bucking, and kicking with its hind legs. These are its basic instinctive responses.

Horses are also extremely sensitive. Their bodies pick up changes in your energetic vibration, which helps them read your intention. Small increases in your heart rate or breathing rate are easily felt by a horse and signal an alert. As herd animals, they specialize in reading the vibrations of fear and danger and recognizing threatening body language (e.g., direct eye contact). An alert from one horse in a herd can send the entire group running for safety.

The horse reacts to the most powerful energy in its environment. The energy draws the horse in, dictating its emotional state and behavior. To be an effective leader, you must be this energy.

The horse uses its entire being as a sensor to evaluate its environment and make decisions. It assesses the physical environment and reads energy and intention. In my equine-assisted coaching sessions, I teach my clients to do the same. These are powerful tools for successful leadership. We begin with self-awareness. Here's the scene in my "office."

In each session, the horse is loose in an enclosed arena. Our sessions are conducted unmounted (i.e., no riding), and the horse is free to move about at will. No horse experience is necessary. Sometimes we perform a couple exercises outside of the arena before we enter the space with the horse. For example, I help you notice where you are holding stress in your body, identify and shift the focus of your attention to various body parts, and practice deep breathing and releasing tension. During this time, the horse is observing your energy and intention, working to determine if you are a threat and reflecting back your state of mind.

This feedback appears physically in the horse, and each horse's response is unique. For example, if you are nervous, the horse reads this emotion as fear—a threat. Something has challenged your emotional and/or physical safety. This emotion is quite real to the horse and elicits a danger alert. The horse may reflect your nervousness by walking as far away from you as possible. Or it may stand still in one place, its butt facing you, and appear to hold its breath. Or the horse may run around the arena, shake its head, or buck or rear. Or it may refuse to look in your direction. It may show a combination of these behaviors or even something entirely different. It depends on the horse and what stirs it that day.

But as soon as you relax and breathe deeply, the horse will exhale reflecting your release of tension. It may stop and look at you. If the horse was running, it may walk. The horse will drop its head lower to the ground and may lick its lips. It will appear to relax as you relax. Some horses will walk right up to you, reflecting your relaxed state as safe and free of threat. The horse becomes the physical manifestation of the energy you hold and your emotional state.

But horses are not the only ones who reflect emotions. Humans also respond to the most powerful energy around them and often reflect the corresponding emotions of that energy. This is a form of energetic entrainment; individuals unconsciously yield their emotions to the most influential energy around them. And we do it every day.

For example, do you listen to music when you're in the car? If so, you often find yourself singing along, feeling happy or sad depending on the lyrics, beat, and rhythm. You become completed immersed in the music, voluntarily entrained by the emotions it evokes, reflecting the intention of the singer. Creative advertising firms capitalize on this concept too, crafting compelling images that elicit strong emotions and make you want to buy. They capture your attention, draw you in with images of excitement and possibility, and provide an incentive to purchase.

In both cases, a powerful energy temporarily controls your emotional state. This happens throughout our daily lives (e.g., politicians leading political rallies, corporate meetings, and even in individual staff or client interactions). At political rallies, the leader incites the crowd, generating anger and outrage to motivate action on an issue. Following a report of low earnings, a corporate leader may give a heartfelt speech to bring confidence to her team. This leader's confidence offers her team the encouragement it needs to move forward; their renewed confidence reflects her intention.

The ability to hold a deliberate intention and influence others is central to leadership success. But surprises can derail intended plans. If you let them.

Here's an example of how a bird's emotional state entrained me and almost compromised my own intention.

At the start of one *Alpha Horse Leadership Training for HUMANS*™ workshop, the group entered the indoor arena with Cali, a calm and quiet experienced horse. I turned Cali loose and addressed the group. Suddenly a black bird flew overhead then slammed into a wall with a bang. He screeched, violently flapped his wings, then flew off across the arena and smacked against another wall. Trapped in the arena, the bird raced back and forth chirping desperately, each time hitting the walls with a thud, his feet scraping the walls in search of footing. Cali freaked. Her tail lifted high over her back, she pranced and snorted, her eyes wide, her veins bulging. We watched the bird in horror, fearful for its life, our emotions entrained by the bird's panic. I realized that the bird was controlling the workshop and that something must be done before he killed himself.

I asked the participants to close their eyes, relax, and breathe deeply with me. To offer Cali and the bird a calm emotional state. To make our calm energy the strongest emotion in the room. We breathed and relaxed and, after about one minute, the bird found a perch and Cali stood still, her eyes quiet. All remained calm after that and the bird eventually found its way out. We had successfully shifted the panicked fear energy to one of peace and calm, and created a safe environment.

The ability to read intention and quickly respond to energy shifts has kept wild horses safe for years. But it can be exasperating for domestic horse owners. For example, most horses won't let you catch them from the field when you're in a rush (even when you have a delicious treat). Your energy reflects your anxious state, triggering the horse's flight response, and it flees. I've had entire herds run from me when I'm late for a riding lesson and trying to retrieve my horse. This also happens with trailer loading. The horse that walked perfectly into the trailer days earlier refuses to load under stress—your stress. It's reading your anxiety as a danger alert and will not follow you without a fight. This is most frustrating, but once you learn to manage your emotional state and become the place of safety for the horse, the problem disappears.

I find that the same is true for humans. As leaders, it's important to make your request or give direction from a place of peace and certainty. But know that people are not always willing to immediately reflect your intention and do your bidding. Their past experiences may keep them from following, and they may be unwilling to give up this history. They don't always shift as quickly as horses!

This takes us to the second reason why horses are so great at teaching emotional intelligence: The horse lives fully in the present. In the now.

The Horse Lives in the *Now*

In nature, horses assess a situation, react, and then resume grazing or sleeping or another relaxed state. Unlike humans, horses don't worry about the future or past situations. Only the present is important. Working with a horse requires that you give your full attention to the present and leave your distractions behind.

This ability to stay fully present allows horses to quickly respond to shifts in your emotional state and intentions. Their speedy physical feedback provides real-time data and gives you an opportunity to see how you are perceived, make adjustments, and optimize your leadership approach. Your success is gauged by how readily the horse responds to your requests.

Horses only willingly follow confident, clear, and congruent leaders. Those with certainty of purpose, commitment, and focus. A horse will never willingly follow a doubtful, scattered, or passive leader. If you are calm, sincere, and clear, the horse will usually follow your lead. If you are nervous or doubtful, the horse will respond in kind, become suspicious and not take your direction. And, if you request one thing, but believe something different in your heart, the horse will reflect this incongruence, and be confused and unable to process the request. The horse is receiving mixed messages.

Giving mixed messages sabotages your leadership. This happens a lot with folks facing subconscious fear issues. The horse will not willingly take your direction no matter your assertion. It sees the fear in your soul. Resolve the fear and the horse will follow. Immediately.

For example, Joan, a self-proclaimed "pushover" at work and home, wanted to build her assertiveness skills. She was tired of people not listening to her. And she was tired of cleaning up after others, doing the work that she had delegated. She wanted more respect. Joan's task was to inspire Cali to walk over a pole on the ground without using a rope.

Joan talked to Cali: "Okay, Cali, let's try to get you over to the pole" and pointed to the pole. Cali looked at the pole. The pole sat about 15 feet away. Joan waved her arms over her head. Cali didn't budge. Joan waved her hands toward Cali and tried again. Cali didn't move. This went on for about 30 minutes, and Joan tried all sorts of enticements: picking up an orange cone, pushing around a red ball, and begging and pleading Cali to move. With each attempt, Cali looked at Joan, her ears pricked up and her eyes bright. Joan had Cali's attention, but the horse refused to move. I intervened and asked Joan a few questions. Our discussion went something like this:

Me: What does "try" mean?

Joan: [looking at me slightly exasperated] Nothing, I guess.

Me: Who do you need to be to inspire her to move?

Joan: Confident.

Me: What else?

Joan: She needs to respect me.

Me: What do you need to do to gain her respect?

Joan: I don't know.

Me: What do you do when you need other people to do things?

Joan: I ask them nicely.

Me: Do they do it?

Joan: Not always.

Me: Then what do you do?
Joan: I usually end up doing it myself. Ah. [heavy sigh]
Me: How do you need to be as a leader to inspire action
        and meet this goal?

Joan looked at me and took a deep breath. She stood up taller, glanced at the pole, and clapped her hands at Cali. Cali walked several steps. Surprised, Joan dashed over to Cali and jogged next to her. Cali stopped and looked at her. Joan took another breath, seemed to grow even taller, and clapped assertively several times as she moved toward Cali. Cali walked toward the pole. About 10 feet from the pole, Cali stopped again and looked at Joan. Joan kept her eyes on the pole and walked toward Cali, exhaling, her arms outstretched. Cali walked easily over the pole. Joan squealed with joy.

This example demonstrates that as long as Joan was sincere, assertive, and committed to her task, Cali would move. No matter that for 30 minutes prior, the horse wouldn't budge. Horses live in the present and respond to who you are *now*. Each moment that Joan stepped into a place of confidence, Cali responded with movement.

The lessons? Be the person you need to be *now* to get results. Take chances. Step out of your comfort zone. Try something new. Break old patterns. Release the past.

The example also shows the importance of awareness of "other." Like people, all horses are different. What inspires one may mean nothing to another. There is no cookie cutter for leadership. You must be adaptable and flexible, and decide what is needed in that moment to best inspire a desired outcome. Joan figured out what Cali needed to respect her and follow her lead. She stepped out of her comfort zone and commanded action. Joan's resolve, energetic intensity, and physical actions were essential to her success.

Your self-awareness blended with an awareness of "other" creates a powerful inspired leader.

The Horse Validates Congruence

This ability to read intention and live in the present makes the horse a perfect mirror for humans to see themselves in action. They read your true intentions and reflect the depth of your soul. They see when you are confused and feeling vulnerable. They know when you are trying to prove something. And they also see your confidence.

One of the most amazing aspects of working with horses is their empathy for our deepest emotions. Cali, who won't give you the time of day when you're "trying" to lead her, is the most sympathetic ear when someone is dealing with raw emotional pain. I believe this is because even though horses move away from fear, they move toward congruence. And when someone is totally honest with himself or herself, the horse validates this honesty. The horse knows when what you think, feel, and say are in alignment. And it physically demonstrates this accord.

For example, my client Dee booked a session to address her "people pleaser" tendencies that prevented her from expressing her own desires and advancing her career. Dee was a high performer, always going above and beyond at work, and although she was recognized for these efforts, she never felt that she did enough. I selected Cali as her partner, and we began with some deep-breathing exercises. Cali stood close to us and exhaled deeply, reflecting Dee's willingness to release her pain. Tears rolled down Dee's cheeks as she expressed her issues. Cali stood next to Dee and breathed softly into her neck. At times, Cali gently touched Dee with her nose. Dee reached out to pet Cali and Cali backed away. Then Cali gently touched Dee again. Dee reached out to reciprocate and again Cali backed away. After a few minutes, I asked Dee a few questions. Our conversation went something like this.

Me: How does it make you feel when Cali touches you?
Dee: Like she understands me. It's such a gift.
Me: How does it feel to be understood?
Dee: Amazing.

M: How does it make you feel when you reach out to touch her and she backs away?

Dee: Like she doesn't want me to pet her.

Me: What does that mean to you?

Dee: That she doesn't want me to touch her in return.

Me: Can you accept her gift without having to give anything in return?

Dee: I feel like I should give her something.

Me: Why?

Dee: Because I am not worthy of her gift.

Me: Then why is she touching you?

Dee laughed and smiled through her tears. A few months after this session, Dee accepted her dream job managing a fast growing firm. She told me that her work with Cali had changed her life.

Why horses validate congruence is a mystery, but I see it repeatedly in my practice. Horses validate your conscious awareness, when you realize and accept the truth about how you really feel. My observations lead me to believe that horses somehow know when your mind, body, and spirit are in alignment. In this place of truth, healing may begin and new options for your life unfold. A horse supports this place of truth by staying close to your side.

A lack of congruence shows up when your mind tells you one thing but your heart and gut say something different. Or, when you refuse to admit something. For example, knowing that you need to confront a staff person or client, but allowing the issue to perpetuate instead of taking action. Not informing corporate board members of a brewing problem. Or, not making the necessary budget cuts to meet financial goals. This causes conflict in your alignment and turmoil in your body. You may become physically ill, or stressed, get frequent headaches, or experience digestive upset. Trouble occurs when your words and actions don't reflect what you know to be true. These are avoidance behaviors and cause a horse to be suspicious and avoid interaction.

I didn't know this when I first started working with horses. I wish I had. I would have made changes in myself a lot sooner.

Key Points/Questions to Consider

Take a moment to look at yourself. Consider the following questions:

- How do you feel right now?

- What is your emotional state?

- What energy are you projecting?

- What impact does this have on others?

- Are you an effective leader? How do you know?

- What shifts can you make to improve your success?

Chapter 3

Secret #1: Use the "Other 90 Percent"

The first secret to inspired leadership is to tap into the "other 90 percent" of your potential. Experts have claimed for years that we use only use a fraction of our potential. In fact, some state that it's about 10 percent or less. No one really knows the precise number. The bottom line is that you have much more power available to you. But where?

Ah, this is one of my favorite secrets. To optimize your potential, you must bring your entire being to your task. I've been tapping into the "other 90 percent" for most of my life, and it's a key factor in my own success and in the success of my clients. And it's easy. You just have to remember to use it.

When you use your "other 90 percent," you achieve your goals faster. You deepen relationships. You position yourself for financial success. You see options. You make good decisions. You take fast action. You are flexible and adapt to changing situations. These are critical elements for success as a leader and to survive in business.

And it works. I know this for sure. Using the "other 90 percent," I've manifested opportunities, jobs, horses, dogs, and clients into my life. And you can do it, too.

In this chapter, we'll clarify what the "other 90 percent" is and how to use it. Then we'll share some examples of how the horses help you empower this skill. It begins with using your entire body as a sensor. Let's get started.

What Is the "Other 90 Percent"?

I define the "other 90 percent" as your entire being—your body and mind working together in awareness. When you tap into your "other 90 percent," you blend input from your body's major nerve centers with input from your mind.

What? Let me explain.

As Robert Cooper pointed out in his book, *The Other 90%,* your body's major nerve centers include your head (brain), your heart, and your gut. Your head is your rational center, your heart is your feeling center, and your gut is your intuition. You get information from all three centers. If you listen. Let's try.

Ask yourself a question and listen for the response in your head, heart, and gut. For example: Should I keep reading this book? What does your head say? What does your heart say? What does your gut say? I hope all three say to "keep reading" since we have a lot of fun information to share!

You can ask your head, heart, and gut all kinds of questions. Your body is a powerful resource. Now let's consider your mind.

Input from your mind includes your intention, beliefs, energetic vibration, and imagination. This is where you begin to direct your "other 90 percent." Your intention helps you to set a goal. Your beliefs influence your decisions and actions. Your energetic vibration moves you along. And your imagination helps you to see possibilities.

When you use the "other 90 percent," you process information from all of these sources and become a more powerful sensor. This boosts your ability to assess your environment, make good decisions, and take the right action toward your goals.

We see evidence of using the "other 90 percent" all the time. For example, when the phone rings, you sometimes "know" who is on the other end (without looking at caller ID!). Or, you think of someone you haven't seen in months and you see him or her at the grocery store later that day. Or, a mother senses her child is ill—before she gets a call from school.

This is all a form of tapping into the "other 90 percent" of your potential. You are feeling the energetic vibration of another. This just happened to me at a conference. I struck up a conversation with the man next to me. As he was talking, I "knew" that he was a recovering alcoholic. His next sentence was that he had just completed a 12-step program. Weird? Maybe, but maybe not.

These kinds of things are often dismissed as coincidence and insignificant. But once you begin to know how to use the "other 90 percent," you can direct it. And that's when the real fun begins!

Let's talk about what you need to do to fire it up.

How to Empower Your "Other 90 Percent"

To direct your "other 90 percent," you need the following elements:

1. Clear intention and ability to visualize the outcome

2. Beliefs that match your intention

3. Action consistent with your intention

4. Adjustments in your approach based on feedback from your three nerve centers (head, heart, gut)

This is an iterative process and requires that you stay in alignment with all elements. If one is off, you risk creating confusion and compromising your power.

For example, let's say Sue wants to earn one million dollars. She sets her intention to earn one million dollars. She thinks she can earn one million dollars, but she's not certain. Sue starts a company and takes action offering her service. She checks in with her head and it warns that she's investing too much money in the new company. She checks in with her heart and it says to follow her passion and keep going. She checks in with her gut and gets a sinking feeling. But she keeps going on the same path. Following her heart. Her business starts to suffer. Clients are not coming. What went wrong?

Aside from tactical errors in her business development, Sue didn't listen to the feedback she was receiving. Her belief system didn't believe that she could earn one million dollars. Her head and gut were raising alarms, but she pressed on. Sue didn't have support from her entire being.

So what does she do? In this case, she must work on her belief system. If she doesn't believe with conviction that she can earn one million dollars, the rest of the process crumbles.

Belief system issues also show up in my work with horses. If your intention aligns with your beliefs and your body's sensory input, the horse will follow your lead. Your head, heart, and gut are in alignment. But if what you intend and what you believe are different, the horse becomes confused and suspicious and refuses to follow you. Just like Sue's business. She was giving mixed messages, and success couldn't follow.

For a horse or human to follow you, you must believe that you can do what you intend to do. Doubt is fear. It indicates a lack of self-confidence. No one follows a doubtful leader. It is too dangerous.

And there are physical reasons why Sue didn't achieve her million-dollar goal. Her brain was not prepared.

Let's take a look at how the latest neuroscience research contributes to tapping into your "other 90 percent."

Neuroscience and the Power of Beliefs

Consider what happens when you have a thought. For example, you see an advertisement on TV for a vacation in Italy. You think, "I would like to go there." Your thought is then influenced by your beliefs. You say, "But, I could never take the time off. I'm too busy. I have all these deadlines. And who would take care of the dog? He's too old to leave in a kennel. And I shouldn't spend the money right now." And you never go to Italy.

What if you had a different belief system? You see the same advertisement and have the same thought: "I would like to go there." But this thought is influenced by different beliefs. Your say, "Work is really busy, but my staff is fantastic. If I plan it out, they could cover for me. I do need a break. My clients would understand." The next thing you know, you're comparing air travel options. And getting excited!

Your belief system is made up of old thought patterns, impressions, conditioning, and programming from childhood. It influences what you believe you can and cannot do. How much risk you are willing to take. Your level of confidence. How much money you believe you can make. And your beliefs have a physical effect on your brain. How?

Your beliefs create neural pathways in your brain. The more you think a certain way, the more you reinforce that neural pathway. If you have been thinking the same way for years, that neural pathway will be super-strong and fast. If your brain has received negative thoughts for many years, this negativity shapes your perspective and can hold you back.

Negative thoughts keep you in a fear-based perspective. In a mild case of fight-or-flight. This is a reaction to threat. Your body begins to prepare for battle or to run. It releases hormones that increase respiration and heart rates, elevate blood pressure, constrict blood vessels, reduce oxygen to the brain, and decrease your ability to think clearly. In a fear-based perspective, you run from opportunities to go on vacation, as shown in the previous example. You make excuses because you're scared. Your conditioning keeps you locked in a negative neural pathway.

However, here's some great news: Recent neuroscience studies show that your brain has "plasticity." This means it can change, produce new neurons, and form new neural pathways. So if you shift your thoughts, your brain will begin to develop new neural pathways, see new options, and learn new things. Researchers found that this occurs throughout your life regardless of age. I guess you can teach an old dog new tricks!

These neuroscience findings support what those of us who are "positive thinkers" have suspected for years: What you think impacts your success. So to optimize your success, you must spend time on your mindset. You must reprogram your belief system to see more possibilities to achieve your goals.

The easiest way to start is with your intention.

What is your intention? Your intention is what you want to happen. The horses show you that your intention must be clear and consistent with your beliefs to be realized.

To shift your belief systems, start with setting your intention to do so. State your intention. For example, say, "I intend to release all negative thoughts." Good. Now let's work on the rest of your mindset.

How to Build a Positive Mindset

Inspired leaders are beacons of positivity. They know the power of positive energy. They understand that your mind is your most important tool for success. Inspired leaders make sure to nurture this tool to optimize its performance. This starts with clearing negativity and raising your positive vibration. Here are some simple ways to build your positive mindset.

5 Tips to Build Your Positive Mindset

1. Police your words. Ditch "can't," "shouldn't," and any negative references to yourself or others.

2. Say at least three things that you are grateful for every day. Make this a ritual.

3. State at least three affirmations daily. For example, I am powerful. I am wealthy. I am healthy.

4. Visualize yourself having achieved your goal. Use all of your senses. What does it feel like? What are you doing? Who is with you? Are you outside or inside? Walk around in your accomplishment. Make this vision as strong as possible.

5. Declare your goal to others. Even if it feels weird. Making a declaration sends your intention to the universe. It is now no longer a secret just inside you. This simple act causes people to see you in a new way and new opportunities begin to open. Your intention is becoming a reality!

Let's talk a bit more about the power of visualization. This is one of the most important tools for goal achievement. And it's a great way to build positive neural pathways.

Use Visualization to Achieve Your Goals

Visualization is a perfect tool to use to reinforce your intention and ensure that you meet your goals.

To visualize, use your imagination. Design a picture of how you want things to be. To make it super-potent, be sure to imagine how you feel as you "live" in your picture. The more vivid your picture and the more intense your emotions, the more impact it will have on your brain. And the more likely it will become a reality.

You can also use visualization for more mundane matters like taking an exam or writing a report. Picture yourself in that moment, answering the questions with ease. A smile on your face. Picture the words flowing onto the page as you complete the report. Push your chair back from your desk. And go home for the night. In your mind.

I used visualization all the time when I showed my horse Dixie in jumping competitions. She was a nervous dominant mare with a habit of spooking at all sorts of obstacles. I imagined our rides the night before the show. But I was nervous even in my mind! I would imagine galloping and jumping, and could feel myself holding my breath and gripping the saddle. Not good. Using visualization, I worked on smoothing out the rides. I practiced jump courses over and over in my mind to be sure that I maintained a nice, even breath and steady feel throughout the ride. This took a while. As I committed to this practice, we grew stronger and stronger as a team and won many competitions.

Athletes know the power of visualization and use it as part of their training. For example, legendary baseball great Hank Aaron used visualization before every game. And his results were impressive! He holds several records including the number of runs batted in. Hank Aaron is considered one of the greatest baseball players of all time.

But you don't have to be an athlete to visualize. Mental rehearsals work for everyone: business leaders, actors, politicians, musicians, and anyone else looking to improve their performance. Visualization is also used for people suffering from pain. It can help the body to relax and relieve the tension associated with pain.

Visualization works well because your mind and body are in harmony with your intention, the picture you are creating. In your imagination, you control your thoughts and feelings. During visualization, your brain releases hormones that relax you and make you happy, like oxytocin and serotonin. In a relaxed state, you can learn and your brain develops new neural pathways.

Now that you have a little background on the technical side, let's see what it looks like in practice with the horses. And a dog!

What the Horses Say

Lisa's Head Game

Lisa, a business owner, requested a session with the horses to hone her leadership abilities. Lisa struggled with decision-making and asking for what she wanted. She was afraid to do the wrong thing, and gathered more and more information on various options. But she couldn't seem to take action. This was leading to overwhelm.

I selected my horse Cali as her instructor. Lisa and Cali and I entered the arena. We did some breathing exercises to get grounded and focused. I placed a white pole on the ground about 20 feet away from Cali. Cali stood still as a statue. I asked Lisa to inspire and motivate Cali to walk over the pole without touching her or using a lead rope. Then I left the arena.

Lisa walked around Cali, stopped several feet from her, extended her arm and tried to get Cali's attention. Cali didn't budge and appeared not to notice Lisa. Lisa walked around the arena, picked up a cone, rolled a ball, and tried to entice Cali to move. Cali didn't budge and her eyes began to close. After several futile attempts to get Cali's attention, I could see Lisa's frustration. I asked her a few questions.

Me: Where are you holding energy in your body?
Lisa: Completely in my head.

Me: How are you breathing?

Lisa: I'm not. I don't think I can get her to move. I don't
        know what to do.

Me: Rebalance your energy to your heart and gut. Set
        your intention and visualize the outcome.

Lisa took a breath, exhaled, and seemed to relax and grow taller. Cali looked at her. Lisa smiled, her eyes wide with surprise. It was the first time the horse had acknowledged her presence. Lisa took another breath, stepped toward Cali, and looked at the pole on the ground. Cali began to move!

Lisa ran up beside Cali her arms outstretched guiding Cali toward the pole. They walked together for several strides. Right in front of the pole, Cali stopped dead. Lisa walked over the pole and looked back at Cali. Cali stood like a statue, still as night, her eyes beginning to close. Lisa made kissing sounds, waved her arms, and begged Cali to move. Cali didn't budge. Lisa looked at me in dismay. I asked a few more questions.

Me: Where are you holding energy in your body and
        how is your breath?

Lisa: Ah. I'm back in my head. I was so excited when
        we starting moving and then I couldn't believe
        that she was actually going to step across the pole.
        That's when she stopped in her tracks. She must
        have felt my doubt!

Lisa took another breath, turned toward Cali, and exhaled. Cali took two steps over the pole and stopped. The pole was now between the horse's front feet and hind feet.

"Oh, for goodness sake!" cried Lisa. "Doubt crept in again at the last minute!" She stood up tall, took another breath, set her gaze straight ahead, and said, "Come on, Cali. Let's do this!" Cali stepped easily across the pole and followed Lisa to the other side of the arena. Whew!

After the session, Lisa shared that the energy she had been using at work was full of doubt and lacked confidence. It was all in her head. Her work with Cali showed all of these issues: a lack of self-trust, focus, and conviction, which prevented Cali from taking her direction. Once Lisa rebalanced her energy through her head, heart, and gut, and set her intention, she became powerful and Cali believed her. Cali gave her the feeling of how she could be and must be to run her business well.

I Believe You Mom! (A Dog Weighs In)

Other animals can also help you tap into your full potential. A client's dog was a big help in the next example. And the results were profound.

One of my executive clients was ready for a new leadership challenge. Her goal? To be a chief executive officer (CEO). Although she had come close to receiving offers from a few different companies and was technically qualified, she had yet to secure her dream position. She hired me polish her interviewing skills.

I reviewed the CEO position description and developed a list of relevant questions. We conducted a mock interview at her home. I was the interviewer. My goal was to assess her responses using head, heart, and gut. I wanted to be sure she was a great fit, and had the strength and conviction to lead the organization.

On her first attempt, she gave credible, articulate responses, but her words felt empty. I didn't trust that she actually believed she was suitable for the position. I felt doubt in my heart. This reflected her own doubt in her responses. She said she was all in her head. I asked her to rebalance her energy through her head, heart, and gut, reconsider her answers, and respond with more conviction. We began again.

This time her answers were better, but I still was not convinced. She sounded like "corporate-speak." Like the many other professionals I had interviewed in my former career as an executive recruiter. They used buzz words and talked about mission, vision, and financial performance with artfully crafted sentences, but only a few candidates ever resonated with me. I needed to do more to help her find her place of power.

So, I led her through a visualization exercise to be sure she could see herself in this CEO position. She took a deep breath, closed her eyes, and imagined the scene. I guided her through a day as CEO picturing all the activities she would conduct and people she would meet. She began to smile and her facial muscles relaxed. She dropped her shoulders and began to breathe from her belly. Then I asked her to open her eyes and we ran through the questions again.

Wow! She responded with conviction. I felt her confidence in my head, heart, and gut. I saw her as the CEO. At that moment, her dog walked over, put his head in her lap, looked into her eyes, and wagged his tail. He had ignored us up to this point. I asked her what she thought about that. She looked at me incredulous and said, "I think he just validated me." Yes, the dog was drawn to her powerful alignment. Shortly thereafter, she was offered the job.

A "Mother's" Intuition

Here's a story for you moms out there who can sense when your child is hurt. Or when your doctor tells you that you're fine and you know that you're not. We need to pay more attention to our intuition and respect its feedback.

My horse Frescoe was suffering from a mild lameness in his right front leg. There wasn't any obvious swelling, and it was tough to tell what was going on. But I had a sense that he was hurt below his knee along the back of his leg. Maybe a strained ligament?

The vet came out to take a look. She poked around his foot, felt his legs, and watched him trot. Then she did some tests to see if the pain was in a joint. Nothing was conclusive, so she suggested starting with a nerve block in his foot and working up his leg to isolate the injury. After she isolated the location, she would do an ultrasound or other test to determine what was going on. This is standard practice and I'd been through it many times with other horses.

Instead of the nerve block process, I asked that she skip straight to the ultrasound to check out the spot behind his knee. The spot that I thought was bothering him. She looked at me suspiciously, as if I was questioning her judgment. I assured her that I supported her approach, but asked her to please humor me and do the ultrasound.

Luckily she's a good-natured sort and pulled out the ultrasound machine. She first shaved the hair from Frescoe's leg to get a clean read. Then she squeezed out some gel, coated his leg, and moved the ultrasound around the area. She found a slight thickening of his ligament indicating a strain.

He had a strained ligament, just as I suspected. His prognosis was good but he needed six weeks of rest before we could get back to riding. Listening to my intuition saved me time and money in vet bills!

Key Points/Questions to Consider

- Set yourself up for success. Check your thoughts and beliefs for hints of doubt, and use the "other 90 percent" to build a positive mindset.

- If you struggle with making a decision, ask your head, heart, and gut, and listen for the responses.

- To achieve a goal, first visualize yourself after you've met it. How are you feeling? Who is with you? What are you doing? Picture yourself telling someone about the process you took to achieve your goal and what helped you the most. Who do you have to be to achieve this goal?

- Set your intention for each day. This helps you stay on track with your goals, see opportunities, and remain in the energy of your choice.

Chapter 4

Secret #2: Find Neutral—
Keep your Ground in Chaos

One of the secrets to leading a successful happy life is to maintain a balanced emotional state to stay relaxed, focused, and productive. In today's fast-paced world, this can be a real challenge. It's easy to become overwhelmed and fall into chaos.

When chaos strikes, your head starts spinning. You can barely keep up with your own life. Your e-mail, text messages, before-work commitments, after-work commitments, commute, and weekend plans blend into a ball of unending responsibilities and start to rule your life. When you're overwhelmed, even fun stuff can seem exhausting. Especially for those of us who are high achievers. At the peak of my own "busy-ness," I struggle to stay at the helm and sometimes find myself a victim of my own to-do list. Even leisure time with the horses seems hard to carve out.

Overwhelm is a form of chaos and in this state you lose power, become reactionary instead of directive, and can quickly start to smother. And your state of overwhelm doesn't just affect you; it actually impacts others, too. The frenetic energy swirling around in your body extends outside your physical self and reaches out, lassoing those around you and affecting their lives.

You can also see overwhelm reflected in your physical environment: clothes scattered around your bedroom, dirty dishes overflowing the sink and spilling onto the counters, your bills mounding into an impressive heap, your hair untidy. It's not a comfortable way to live.

Left uncontrolled, a state of chronic chaos can lead to more serious problems, such as health issues, poor job performance, and relationship drama. It's important to recognize the symptoms early and take immediate action to rebalance your life.

But how? By rebalancing your energy and finding what I call your "neutral" space. This is the emotional space where you are grounded and connected to the earth energy. You have plentiful oxygen, leave worries behind, and live fully present. You are able to make a move in any direction you choose.

This is one of the best lessons I've learned from horses and I use it every day. It is absolutely essential for success in anything you pursue. In this chapter, we'll discuss this awesome state and how to find it. You'll also see how the horses show you when you're in it, and when you're not!

What Is the "Neutral" Space?

Your neutral space is a place of peace. Your head is quiet and your body is calm yet alert. You are in a relaxed state of being.

Top athletes use the neutral space all the time, knowingly or unknowingly. You can see it physically. They adopt a readiness position, both feet firmly on the ground spaced about shoulder's width apart or farther. Knees relaxed, shoulders loose, their center of gravity in perfect alignment. Their breathing is steady, eyes watchful and expectant. Their mind is calm and alert.

Horses find the neutral space naturally. Watch a herd of horses grazing in a grassy field. They are peaceful, relaxed, and acutely aware of their environment. They are completely in the present—in the *now*. This is their neutral space.

You can also see the neutral space at work. It occurs when you are calm and focused on a task. It also happens in meetings when all are focused on a common goal and everyone is contributing. The leader of the meeting welcomes all input without judgment. This creates a safe environment and generates high productivity.

In my corporate career, I offered the neutral space to settle the energy during important meetings subject to heated discussions, to negotiate with demanding clients, to discuss ambitious deadlines, and to give negative feedback. And no one knew I was doing anything special. But the effect was visible. The vibe in the room would start to settle; you could see the physical shifts in people's bodies as they released tension, took a breath, and prepared to dive in to a productive meeting.

I learned how to find the neutral space as a survival mechanism for dealing with animals, horses primarily. I've worked with and owned several excitable and abused horses. Many were young ex-racehorses who didn't make it at the track and who were mistreated by humans. They came to me underweight and stressed out with no trust in people.

If I tried to catch one of these horses from the field when I was stressed out, it would feel my unbalanced energy and run. It got worse if I tried to ride the horse when I was in this state (picture rearing, spooking, bucking—nice, huh?). I often ended up on the ground. Yes, the law of gravity always prevails.

Learning how to create a safe space for others to be heard without judgment is a critical leadership skill. It's also essential to sales to ensure that you listen carefully to your prospect's concerns and respond in a manner best suited to his or her needs. It forms the beginning of a trusting relationship. Offering this neutral space is the foundation for all of my work. Here's how to find it.

How to Find the Neutral Space

Finding the neutral space requires self-awareness; our three nerve centers (head, heart and gut) should be clear of chatter and open to receive. The good news is that it's super-easy to find the neutral space. You can do it right now. Let's try.

Find the Neutral Space

- Stand or sit comfortably, take a deep breath, and relax your eyes. Notice where your attention is focused. Notice where you are holding tension. Notice what thoughts are in your head. Now take another deep breath.

- Breathe deep into your belly and give your body permission to release all tension. Bring your awareness to your breathing for 10 seconds. Now bring your awareness to your heart space. Feel your heart beating. Breathe deeply and feel your heart rate start to slow down. Feel your feet on the floor. Wiggle your toes. Again feel your feet on the floor. Feel them balanced and connected to the floor. Breathe deeply and bring your attention back to your belly.

- Relax into this space for a minute or so. This is the neutral space. Now gently open your eyes. Better, right?

You can learn to do this in an instant with one breath. It just takes practice.

So let's see how the horses teach this to folks.

What the Horses Say

Mike Finds Neutral

Mike is a successful marketing executive with his own firm. We met at a local event, and he thought it would be "cool" to come out and work with the horses. Since he had no horse experience at all, I selected my calm senior equine instructor, Candlelight, aka "the Cali Lama." Mike and Cali and I walked down to the indoor arena and I let Cali loose in the round pen, an enclosed area that spans half of the area. Mike and I stayed on the outside and observed Cali's behavior.

She traveled around the ring, sniffed the barrels, cones, poles. Then she moved to the center of the ring and stopped facing away from us. Then she slowly walked farther and farther away until she hit the wall of the arena. She looked out the window, appearing totally disinterested in our presence. I asked Mike what he observed about her behavior and what he thought it could mean. He responded, "Maybe she doesn't like me? Maybe she's afraid of me? Maybe she knows that I'm a little afraid of horses? I don't know what she's thinking!"

I asked him if he believed that he was influencing her behavior or if it could be something else. "Oh," he responded, "I guess it doesn't have to be about me. Maybe she just wanted to look out the window. I was assuming that it was something about me." It could be about you, or us, or something entirely different, I added. It's just good to consider various options and avoid assumptions.

We then practiced finding the neutral space. We turned our backs to the ring and stood quietly. I asked him to notice how he felt and where in his body he may be holding tension. He said he felt nervous and excited. And that he felt a little tightness in his shoulders and knees. We then proceeded with the previous exercise to find the neutral space. I could hear Mike breathing deeply and settling in to his feet.

Partway through the exercise, I heard Cali's footsteps. Mike and I stayed in the "neutral" space for a bit, and then I asked him to open his eyes. He said he felt relaxed and centered and much more grounded. I asked him to turn around and look for Cali. She was directly behind us, her nose inches from our back, standing quietly. He was totally surprised. She appeared calm yet interested in our presence, as if we now were a team of three.

Cali was drawn to the neutral energy created by Mike and me, and served as the physical reflection of his emotional state. This balanced state is non-threatening, even inviting, and is the beginning of setting the stage for a productive session.

You can use the neutral space exercise to find your ground no matter what the situation. It starts with a decision to let go of the tension, the thoughts that spin in your head and affect the body. Once you give yourself permission to release the tension, even for a moment, your body can relax. I always tell folks that they can go back and pick up the tension later, but that for the moment, to allow themselves to experience the neutral space. The neutral space sets the foundation for anything-a fresh approach, new learning, new relationships, whatever you desire.

Another way to use the neutral space is to keep your ground in chaos. Working with a client and my horse Lila shows what you need to do when chaos strikes.

Lila Goes Crazy!

Chaos stems from fear. One morning a former senior executive client came out to work with me and Lila. The winter white from a sudden storm blinded us as we made our way to the indoor arena. As we entered the arena, snow and ice slid down from the roof of the building and landed with a thud outside. Lila lost her mind. She reared, spun, and leaped in the air, and it was all I could do to get her safely in the round pen. I asked the client to stay outside the round pen as I secured the gate. Lila raced around the arena, head high, tail up over her back, and eyes wild. Snow kept sliding in chunks down from the roof, and each time she jumped higher, kicking out with her hind legs at invisible foes. Panicking, she sideswiped me a couple of times as she raced by, not even seeing me. Luckily I have a pretty quick side step and avoided a blow.

I could feel her heart beating in my heart, fast, reckless, her breaths short. Her energy was so strong that I could feel it in my own body and had to work to not get absorbed in her fear. I found my neutral space and worked to stay in my own energy, breathing into the neutral space while keeping a lookout for flying hooves. I then expanded my neutral space to beyond my body and out to the full arena, to create a safe space for Lila to calm down. I kept my movements small, just focused on my breathing, and set an intention for peace. When fear takes over a horse, you cannot respond in kind since making a big move adds energy to an already-volatile mix. They cannot hear you when they are in this state. It's like a human who is hysterical or someone frozen by fear.

You also must keep the energy moving forward so it has a place to go and doesn't explode. So, little by little I encouraged Lila to move in different places around the ring, just small moves to guide her, to give her support to work through her fear energy. My job was to gently guide her and be a firm wall for her transformation to neutral. And take whatever time it would take to follow through to that state.

She eventually slowed down, started to "see" me and seek the direction. I asked her to circle around cones, move away from me, and eventually she took a deep breath and walked quietly around the arena, her head hung low, her eyes quiet. She had given herself over to the neutral space, the bigger energy in the room. And what about my client? She said the demonstration was good enough for her and seemed quite relieved not to have to enter the ring!

Key Points/Questions to Consider

The examples with the horses show you how important it is to be aware of the energy you carry and project. Neutral energy can be used at any point to calm yourself and others, and inspire a feeling of safety and trust. Here are a few questions to consider:

- What energy are you holding now?

- Where are you holding tension?

- Take a breath and find the neutral space. What does it feel like?

- Look around your environment. What energy are others carrying? Is their energy affecting you? Is your energy affecting them?

- Stay in your neutral space and interact with another person. How does it feel?

Begin to become aware of the energy you carry throughout the day. If you start to feel stress and overwhelm, take a few minutes and find the neutral space. The more you practice, the faster you will find this peaceful state.

Chapter 5

Secret #3: Trust and Be "Attractive"

Inspired leadership starts with trust. The more you trust yourself, the more trust you have to offer and the more others will trust you.

The most inspired leaders are also magnetic. People flock to hear them talk and hang on their every word. Their books are bestsellers. Their followers are loyal. And this is great for their business!

Just look at Oprah, Apple's Steve Jobs, and the Dog Whisperer, Cesar Millan. All have attracted huge loyal followings.

As a leader, trust empowers you to take chances, discover new opportunities, and build relationships. Others are drawn to your confidence and vision.

Inspired leaders know that success is based on relationships. And all relationships begin with trust. Your relationships form the foundation of your reputation. A great reputation is priceless.

In contrast, when trust is lacking, businesses have high employee turnover rates, low or mixed earnings, and an inconsistent client base. You see frequent changes in leadership and staff, and partnerships crumble. The impact on Lance Armstrong's empire after he confessed to using performance enhancing drugs was financially devastating. It shows the perils of deceit. People lose confidence and flee.

Horses also run when they detect a lack of confidence. They also have a unique ability to know when someone is being "false." Pretending to be something he or she is not. Horses detect this incongruence, feel unsafe, and move away.

47

If you win the trust of a horse, it is drawn to you. You become "attractive" and it will follow you. However, to maintain your attractiveness, you must be compelling and have something great to offer. For a horse, this could be as simple as a feeling of safety. You'll see this in the stories that follow.

But you may have to do a little more to be attractive to humans!

So how do you gain trust and make yourself magnetic? In this chapter, we'll discuss trust and share tips for enhancing your magnetism. Then we'll look at examples of how the horses show you the way. Let's begin by considering trust.

What Is Trust?

People follow and buy from those they know, like, and trust. But what does it mean to trust? It means to feel safe. It means you're confident that you're doing the right thing or following the right person.

However, trust is not an absolute. It builds over time and can be destroyed in an instant. Everyone has a different threshold of trust based on their past experiences and general nature. Some trust more readily than others. As a leader, you must be able to gauge another's level of trust and gain his or her confidence to ensure that he or she follows you.

A level of trust can fluctuate depending on circumstances. For example, someone may purchase a product one day when he is feeling confident and return it the next. He lost trust in his decision. This happens all the time with politicians running for office. You feel confident in a candidate until you hear on the news that she voted against a bill you supported. You're shocked and start looking for someone else to support. Never assume that you have the trust of another.

So before you ask others to follow you or buy from you, firm up their trust level. Give them a call, invite them to lunch, send them a free sample, or do something else to reach out and re-establish your bond. With those that know and like you, this may not take much time, but don't overlook this step.

Also consider the size of the risk you are asking someone to take.

Accepting a bigger risk requires more trust and confidence in you. Make sure you have his or her trust before inviting someone to spend more money or do something he or she has never done before. As a leader, you must make people feel safe and confident, or they may flee! And their trust in you erodes.

When you gain a high level of trust, you begin to be "attractive." Others start to notice you. Let's explore what it means to be "attractive" as a leader. And I'm not talking about your good genes or wardrobe!

What Is Attraction?

In terms of inspired leadership, to "attract" is to draw, maintain, and influence another's attention. To keep someone's focus on you. In business, attraction is founded on an excellent reputation. Your clients are happy and tell others. Word spreads and new prospects contact you. You become sought after and irresistible. And people want to work for you.

And your passion for your work is obvious. Others are drawn to you. Inspired by your energy and confidence. You don't feel like you're selling. But you are.

This is something I call "authentic sales." And it's key to being attractive. You are selling from the heart.

As Robert Cooper mentions in his book, *The Other 90%*, research shows that your heart energy is the most powerful energy emitted from your body. And as we discussed in Chapter 4, people's emotions are influenced by the biggest energy around them. When you believe in something, you become passionate. Your passion—your heart energy—becomes the dominant energy. It's contagious and draws others in.

When you practice "authentic sales," you engage your heart energy. You know the value that your product or service provides, you believe in it, and you're excited to share it. Proof of its value is found in feedback and testimonials from happy clients. You have positively impacted their lives. You invite others to try it with confidence. Certain it will help.

When you practice "authentic sales," what you think, feel, say, and do are in harmony. You are congruent in your head, heart, and gut (as we discussed in Chapter 3). And this makes you powerful.

If you consistently provide a great product or service, your name and brand become associated with trust and reliability, which are quite attractive. This is how brand loyalty develops. Your brand becomes a symbol of trust and proven performance. It draws others to you.

You see brand loyalty all over the world. From automobiles like Subaru and BMW, to facial tissue like Kleenex, and athletic shoes like Nike. Each of these entities is known for providing consistent value to their clients. Their attraction is strong.

Attraction relies on congruence. It will sputter out if you don't believe what you're saying. If what you think, feel, say, and do are not in agreement, conflict will be created between your head, heart, and gut. This conflict resonates out creating confusion and doubt. Others will lose confidence and your attractiveness wanes.

Horses pick up your level of confidence and reflect how you feel in your head, heart, and gut. It's easy to see your attractiveness when you work with a horse. They either ignore you or want to be with you. This begins with your ability to get their attention.

Getting the attention of a horse is similar to trying to get the attention of a person. Some take more enticing than others. Like people, they also get distracted. I've never seen a human be more attractive than a bucket of grain! This doesn't mean they don't trust you. You're just not the main attraction at the moment.

This can happen in business as well. Staff get distracted with competing priorities, other people, and even their home life. As a leader, it's your job to refocus their attention on you, their responsibilities, and the project objectives. In sales, you must get your prospects thinking about you and your great stuff.

You know you're attractive when your staff, colleagues, and clients choose to stay with you. They trust you and know your greatness. It's a wonderful feeling.

So where do you begin? First, you must get someone to notice you. You must get their attention and be worth their time. Let's look at what this means.

Importance of Full Attention

To be attractive, you must give your full attention to your target. Are you listening?

Consider the following questions:

- When is the last time you gave your full attention to someone or something? What did it feel like?

- When is the last time someone gave you their full attention? What did that feel like?

To receive someone's full attention is a gift. You feel special. You feel heard. And it's rare.

In today's hectic world of buzzing cell phones and overpacked schedules, giving and getting full attention can be a challenge. Why?

Because to give and receive full attention, you must slow down, listen, and acknowledge another. Your head, heart, and gut must be clear of chatter and open to receive. When you give your full attention, you are quiet in your head, open in your heart, and receiving in your gut. This is the place where a true connection begins.

And who has time for that? I'm kidding, of course. But I did get your attention, right?

When you have someone's full attention, he or she looks directly into your eyes and leans forward. The same is true for horses. They look you in the eye, their ears pricked forward in interest.

Inspired leaders know how to encourage this connection and attract others to them. They know how to be worth your attention because they believe they are worth your attention. And that you are worth their attention.

This is reflection. Just as horses reflect your emotional state (as we discussed in Chapter 2), other people can reflect your truth. What you really believe. If you don't feel worth their attention, they won't give it to you. Interesting, eh?

And individuals respond differently to a call to attention; what works for one may not work for another. You must be able to offer various approaches.

To become attractive, you must be able to keep their attention. You must be worthy of their time and interest. This can be tricky.

It all starts with you.

Building trust and creating an attractive force takes time. Let's take a look at some specific ways to draw others to you. And then we'll see what the horses say.

How to Build Trust and Be Attractive

The first step in building trust and creating an attractive force is to take an honest look at yourself. At the energy you hold and how your nonverbal communication influences the vibration you give off and how others see you.

Fear-based energy drives others away. Confidence and positivity attract. Consider the following questions in your head, heart, and gut:

- Do you trust yourself?

- Do you trust others?

- Do you believe in what you do?

- Are you great at what you do?

You must trust yourself before others will trust you. If you do not trust others, you will give off fear-based energy and they won't trust you. Create a positive mindset to shift out of fear (as we discussed in Chapter 3).

As you trust yourself and others, you gain more confidence and you attract more followers. However, creating an attractive force is not a passive process. Unfortunately you can't just sit around radiating positive energy! To draw others to you, you must take specific action. We'll talk about that in a moment.

Here's the great news: Once you begin to generate this attraction, it gains more and more momentum, drawing more prospects and opportunities to you. Social media illustrates this attractive force at work. If my good friend "likes" a business on Facebook, I'll probably "like" it, too. At a minimum, I'll take a look.

People hang around others with similar interests. It goes back to the fact that people follow and buy from those they know, like, and trust. Referrals shortcut the trust-building process even more. If my friend was happy with your service, I'll be more inclined to hire you than someone else. Trust by association helps empowers your attraction.

Let's look at how you can build your attractive force.

10 Tips to Build Attractiveness

1. Have great stuff to offer. No one will give you their full attention without getting something in return. What are you offering? What would interest them? Why should they care about what you're saying? In business, this means that you must be great at something! You must be able to claim expertise as the "go-to" firm. This will draw clients and attract great employees.

2. Believe in your stuff. People are drawn to those who speak with conviction. Those with certainty. Those with confidence. You must be certain that your stuff is great, or people will sense that you're not confident in it. If it needs a little tweaking, tweak it. If you need to consult an expert for help making it even better, hire the expert. Or take a class to be sure that you stay on top of your game. Claim your greatness; no one else will claim it for you.

3. Focus and give your full attention. The ability to focus is key to being attractive. You must be able to give something or someone your full attention and know what this feels like. People know when you are distracted and your distraction causes them to lose focus and their mind starts to wander.

Distraction is a form of competition. Something else is competing for your attention or the attention of your people. The most compelling leaders keep their people riveted. How? Keep reading.

4. Connect and engage. Reach out to your staff and clients. Get to know them. Ask for their opinion; value their input. Show them you care. Bring them together through online groups or your Facebook page, and host a gathering. The more people see others that love your work, the closer they feel to you. It validates their choice and makes them feel good about their decision.

5. Know what they want, need, and are willing to pay for. Know your target market. Spend time surveying them and review their feedback. The best companies in the world stay in close contact with their clients and anticipate their needs. They show up first with an offer and stay ahead of their competition. This also applies to your staff. Know the needs of your staff. Know what will motivate them to give you their best. Check in regularly (outside of the annual performance review). Make sure they are able to use their best strengths and keep them connected to your overall goal. Share the vision.

6. Be visible with your great stuff. "Out of sight, out of mind." We've all heard that phrase before. You must show up consistently in places where your clients and prospects can see and hear you. Trust builds over time. Seek opportunities to share your expertise so others get to know you. Create videos and audios, and give talks for free. Show up online as an expert. Comment in social media groups. Conduct interviews and offer insights. Create a presence. Focus your paid advertising where your people will see it (e.g., industry trade journals and special online groups). And ask for testimonials; they are fabulous social proof. Share them with the world!

7. Trust. Trust yourself and others. Keep your promises. Honor your word. To yourself and others. Start small. If you tell yourself that you will work out each day, do it. Even on days when you're really busy, just do 10 minutes of something. Wake up 10 minutes earlier if you have to. If you have to draft a report, do it. Put other things aside, turn off the phone and e-mail, and work on the report uninterrupted for a specific amount of time. These simple activities begin to build your confidence, trust, and focus.

8. Recognize others. Recognize staff members who are doing great work, colleagues on the cutting edge of your industry, and clients for their work. Also recognize and support other groups you believe in (e.g., nonprofits). A social conscious is very attractive.

9. Ask for the sale. Many businesses offer great products and services but fail to ask for the sale. Or they feel uncomfortable about the sales process. I believe that if you have something great to offer and you believe your prospect could benefit, it is your responsibility to invite them to buy your stuff. They can always say no. But if you refuse them an opportunity to consider your stuff as an option, you are cheating them out of a chance to improve their lives.

10. Give back. Donate your time, expertise, and/or financial resources to causes you support. Even giving a little bit of time for another in need can yield a huge impact. And it makes you feel great. Which raises your positive vibration and expands your attractiveness. But do it because you want to do it, not because you feel you "should." Your head, heart, and gut will know your true motivation!

Now that you're positively irresistible, let's look at what the horses say about trust and attracting what you desire.

What the Horses Say

Charlie Takes a Nap!

Nina, a successful entrepreneur, was struggling with a relationship that was starting to affect her focus at work. She brought her horse, Charlie, out for a session to explore new communication strategies and learn more about emotional intelligence.

We walked into the arena, turned her horse loose, and sat across from each other in two chairs. Charlie walked around the space sniffing the sand. Nina and I started our conversation. Charlie stayed on the far end of the arena while Nina shared her frustration.

Nina and I did a couple of breathing exercises to calm her energy. Charlie walked over while we breathed, sniffed us, licked the chairs, and ambled around the arena. Then Nina exhaled deeply and we resumed our conversation. Charlie also exhaled and wandered back to where we were sitting.

As Nina spoke, Charlie walked up behind my back, put his head on my shoulder, and peered across at his owner. She kept talking and ignored the giant head on my shoulder. His head was pretty heavy! Then he lifted his head and put it on my other shoulder and stared at Nina. I almost laughed. She kept talking. Charlie took a deep breath and laid down in the sand at our feet. He slept for about 20 minutes flat out on his side while we talked. Laying down in a strange place is an extremely vulnerable position for a horse.

I asked Nina what she thought about his behavior. She said that he seemed to feel very safe with me and that when he put his head on my shoulders, he looked like he wanted to see her from my perspective. She also mentioned that perhaps he was showing her that it was okay to relax and that she was safe.

I agree. After we rebalanced Nina's energy, Charlie was attracted to our space and trusted that they were both safe. He demonstrated this by being fully vulnerable. It was an honor to receive this level of trust from a horse.

Joe Lives in the Now

Mary brought her husband, Joe, to a session to deepen their relationship. Joe had suffered a stroke a few years earlier, which had been stressful and difficult for them both. Joe had recovered well physically but still experienced weakness along his left side. Mary thought some time with the horses would be a fun activity to strengthen their marriage. I selected my horse Lila to work with Joe.

Although Joe had never touched a horse before, he was fearless. I asked him where his energy was focused and he said, "Throughout my body." The objective of his session was to connect with Lila, feel her energy, and just be together.

Joe picked up a cone on the ground and offered it to Lila. She accepted the offer and chewed gently on the end of the cone. Then he rolled a big red exercise ball toward Lila. She reached out and touched it with her nose, her ears pricked with curiosity, her eyes watching Joe's every move.

Since he clearly had her attention, I asked Joe to lead Lila around the arena without a rope, using his energy and intention. He picked up an orange riding stick and tapped it on the ground in front of him. Lila walked up on his weaker side, her nose near the ground sniffing the end of the stick. Then they fell in step together and Joe guided Lila all over the arena. She stuck like glue to his side and followed him everywhere. When they were done, Joe was awestruck. Mary was thrilled, a huge smile spread across her face. Joe's absolute trust in himself and Lila had created a beautiful partnership. At the end, Joe thanked Lila and she nuzzled her head in his chest.

Joe gave Lila his full attention and he received her full attention in return. His curiosity, balanced emotional state, and sense of exploration and play drew Lila to him. His fearlessness allowed him to experience the magic of the present moment.

Julie Builds Self-Trust

Julie struggled with fear issues following a riding accident years before, and had lost confidence in herself and her riding. She brought her horse, Midnight, to work on their relationship. Midnight, a young horse, was tense and spooky, which further triggered Julie's anxiety. Julie feared that her lack of confidence was getting worse and damaging their relationship.

Before entering the arena, we stood outside the gate with Midnight and practiced deep breathing. The mare stood still, her breath shallow, her eyes wide and staring. I could feel Julie's energy in my own body; I felt a tightness in my chest, tension in my head, and no awareness of my lower body. Julie confirmed that this was how she felt.

I asked Julie to bring her attention to her feet, feel their connection to the ground, wiggle her toes, and release tension in her knees and hips. And to continue to breathe deeply. Julie exhaled and Midnight turned her head to look at her indicating that Julie was starting to relax. Then we all entered the arena.

As Julie and I stood together, I explained the importance of using her entire body as a sensor and how horses reflect our emotional state. Midnight initially stood next to us, but then walked a few steps away and sniffed the ground. Then she returned to where we were standing. She did this a few times. I asked Julie some questions. Our conversation went something like this:

Me: What do you make of Midnight's behavior?

Julie: She's insecure.

Me: Are you insecure?

Julie: Yes, in my relationship with her.

Me: What else could her behavior mean?

Julie: Maybe she's curious.

Me: And what does that mean?

Julie: That she is starting to gain confidence and explore.

Me: What else?

Julie: I don't know.

Me: Are you and I a safe place in this arena?

Julie: Yes, we could be.

Me: Why?

Julie: Because we give her confidence.

Me: Why?

Julie: [smiling] Because we are confident.

Just this small shift in perspective allowed Julie to consider new options to explain Midnight's behavior and remove her fear-based label of "insecure." I left the arena, and asked Julie to play with her new confidence and walk together with Midnight around the arena without the lead rope.

At first Midnight walked away from Julie. Julie walked behind her and followed her around the arena. Then Midnight stopped dead. She held her body still and refused to look at Julie. Her eyes stared straight ahead. I asked Julie where she was holding her energy and how she was feeling. She said her energy was in her chest and she was a bit nervous. She had lost confidence.

I suggested that she breathe, reconnect with her body, and trust herself. She took a breath and Midnight walked by her side, drawn to her confidence and trusting her leadership. They walked side-by-side around the arena without a rope. When they were done, Julie was beaming. "How was that?" I asked. "Awesome!" she replied.

Midnight was attracted to this self-trust, the new confidence that Julie exuded.

Key Points/Questions to Consider

- What does full attention look like?

- How does it feel to give someone your full attention?

- How does it feel to receive the full attention of another?

- What is required to give or receive full attention?

- Positive energy attracts. Fear-based energy repels. Which do you project?

- Do you believe in your greatness? Are you sure? What do you need to gain more confidence?

- Go out there and claim your greatness!

Chapter 6

Secret #4: Use the Power of Comfort Zones

One of the most important secrets of inspired leadership is to understand and use the power of comfort zones. Your comfort zone is the emotional and physical space in which you feel completely safe. Your personal "bubble" of safety. In your bubble, you are calm, trusting, process information clearly, and perform your tasks with ease. You are relaxed and focused. Outside of this space, you begin to get nervous.

Inspired leaders know their comfort zone and recognize the comfort zones of others. They understand that if you push someone outside of his or her comfort zone, you may get negative results. For example, if you're negotiating a deal and your prospect starts to squirm in his chair and avoid eye contact, you may be pushing too hard. If you continue what you're doing, you risk hearing a "no." And he may dart for the door!

The same can happen with staff. If they get pushed beyond their comfort zone too often, they lose confidence. Mistakes occur, absenteeism may rise, and you risk losing them.

Here's the tricky part about comfort zones: They are elastic. They expand and contract depending on the confidence level of the person and the circumstance. Just because someone felt one way one day doesn't mean she'll feel the same way the next day. Her bubble today may be bigger than tomorrow. You must search for slight shifts in energy and body language for clues. We'll talk about this in a moment.

Horses also show the ever-changing nature of comfort zones. For example, if one encroaches on another's space in the field, the violator may get bit or kicked. The comfort zone boundary is clear. But the next day the same two horses graze nose to nose. Like best friends. Their comfort zones now include each other.

Your comfort zone expands with confidence, trust, and experience. I learned a lot about comfort zones from horses. For example, when I was teaching my horse Dixie to jump into water, she was terrified at first. She would stand at the edge of the water her body aquiver. Then she'd reach down, sniff the water, snort, and run backward. Gradually she put a toe in and then another toe, and we'd "tiptoe" through the water. She'd splash out on the other side all proud. But if I pushed her when we first approached the water, she would stop dead, panic, and refuse to go in. It took patience and time.

As your comfort zone grows, it empowers you to inspire others to follow you. They feel your confidence and trust you to guide them. They trust you to take them forward through their fears. To do this successfully, you must be aware of their emotional state from moment to moment. Listen to their feedback and make changes to your approach. And take them step-by-step to build confidence. Like teaching a child to walk. Or teaching a horse to go through water!

The best leaders do this naturally. They know how much to push and when to back away. They respect personal boundaries—the line that if crossed violates trust. Their sales conversions are high and their staff are top performers.

Inspired leaders also know when to stand their ground and let someone be uncomfortable. They stay supportive yet firm until the other relaxes or walks away. This skill is handy for managing "high-maintenance" clients. You know the type: After you've signed an agreement, they change their mind. You accommodate them. They change their mind again and ask for more—and expect you to do it for no extra fee by the original deadline. Each time you meet their request, they want more. And with each request, they push against your comfort zone. Respect on both sides erodes. But once you stand your ground, the boundary becomes clear. By finding the edge of your comfort zone, they know your limit and back down.

Reading comfort zones requires a keen awareness of self and other, and attention to nonverbal communication and energy. The more accurate you are at reading your own bubble, the more self-aware you become. And the better you will be able to read others and use this skill to meet your goals.

This skill can be used to guide prospects through the sales process, lead staff, and negotiate agreements. It's also great for working with horses; you don't want to misread a cue from a 1,200-pound animal!

In this chapter, we'll dive a little deeper and look at how to tell when you may have stepped over a line and violated trust. We'll also highlight 10 tips for using the power of comfort zones. And then you'll see what the horses say on the topic.

Comfort Zones at Work

Comfort zones are not visible, and everyone's is different. As I mentioned, they also expand and contract with your confidence. Even on the same day. You may be confident in the morning, embrace new challenges, and take on new activities. But by afternoon, you're nervous about meeting with a new client and your guard is up. You wonder what the heck you've committed to!

So let's break it down. There is your physical comfort zone—the physical distance at which you tolerate another's presence. And your emotional comfort zone—the level of trust and intimacy you feel with another. Both can be felt by others, but most feel this subconsciously.

As someone approaches the edge of your comfort zone, either physical or emotional, your body has a physical response. A fear response. You heart beats a bit faster, your breathing begins to elevate, or you hold your breath. You begin to feel threatened—unsafe. Someone is about to violate a boundary. This feeling may be strong or mild, but it's there.

The problem is that this tense emotional state reduces your ability to think clearly. To listen and make good decisions. This isn't good for either party. And it's bad for business interactions.

The funny thing is that this fear response can be triggered by common office activities. For example, someone stands too close to you, barges into your office, talks loudly, interrupts you or talks over you, or touches you to get your attention. Or perhaps they send you an email asking you to do something urgent without first checking if you're available. All people have different levels of sensitivity. What is perceived as a comfort zone violation to one has no effect on another. You may not have any idea that you violated another's boundary.

So let's take a look at some signs that you may be getting too close.

What it Looks Like When You Hit the Edge of a Comfort Zone

Getting close to the edge of someone's comfort zone elicits physical and emotional reactions. The physical signs vary, but common ones include the following:

1. Arms crossed over chest

2. Backing up or leaning away from you

3. Avoiding eye contact - looking down, away, or over your head for someone else

4. Fidgeting - wiggling in chair, fiddling with hands or hair

5. Heavy sighs

6. Checking watch

7. Talking faster or not talking

8. Nodding and smiling more than normal

9. Sweating palms (e.g., rubbing hands on pants!)

10. Swallowing or sipping a lot of water or coffee

11. Turning torso away from you and toward the exit

12. Making an excuse to leave

Emotional reactions are more difficult to discern. This is where you have to rely more on your intuition. Ask yourself the following questions and listen for the responses in your head, heart, and gut (as we discussed in Chapter 3):

1. How do I feel?

2. Does she feel the same way? How do I know? What are the signs?

3. How would I feel if I were her?

4. Is she matching how fast I talk or is she talking faster or slower?

5. Is she looking me in the eye?

6. Does she appear interested?

7. Does she trust me? How do I know?

When people trust each other and are connected, they talk at about the same pace, use similar voice inflections, and look each other in the eye. They use open body language: Their shoulders are relaxed, their hands rest at their sides or on the desk, and their torsos face each other. They keep their full attention on each other. When you have that connection, you can start to build a strong relationship for any endeavor.

Now that you know what reactions to prevent and what you're aiming for, let's consider how you can use the power of comfort zones to raise your game.

How to Use the Power of Comfort Zones

Once you understand comfort zones, you can use this knowledge to set yourself up for success. To get the best out of your staff or close a sales deal, you must be able to make them feel safe so they can think clearly, make good decisions, and feel great about working with you.

The following tips can be used for sales conversations, meetings with colleagues, negotiations, and leading your team. Just remember that every person has unique comfort zone preferences. You'll have to watch carefully to get a sense of the other's preferred physical and emotional distance and not approach too close too early.

10 Tips for Using the Power of Comfort Zones During a Meeting

1. Identify your own comfort zone and energy before the other person arrives. Consider how you are feeling. Are you nervous, excited, or distracted? Are you confident? The other person will read your energy at a subconscious level. And your energy will elicit a positive, negative, or a neutral response.

2. Get calm and find the "neutral space," as we discussed in Chapter 4. Offering neutral energy creates a calm productive environment.

3. Sit across from each other. Sitting side-by-side is awkward and makes eye contact difficult, and the closeness can make someone nervous. If you're standing next to each other, position yourself about an arm's length away to begin. Stand with your body at a slight angle to the other person, not directly facing him or her. Standing face-to-face can be confrontational. You can always adjust as you both gain trust.

4. Keep your body language open, your shoulders relaxed, your arms on the table or relaxed at your sides. Smile and look the other person in the eye.

5. Ask questions to hear their thoughts and gain insights. This

will also help confirm the agenda for the meeting. Don't assume that the agenda you discussed earlier is still in play; the other person may have a more pressing need or something else that they wish to discuss. It's more important to create a positive experience than to seal a deal.

6. Pay attention to your emotional state and energy at all times. If you feel nervous or begin to get angry, take a breath and go back to neutral. You may be picking up energy from the other person. It is important to stay neutral to listen and respond appropriately. Stay focused on making the other person comfortable. If she gets upset, be sure to stay in neutral to remain the leader. Be empathetic to what the other person may be experiencing but avoid getting drawn into drama.

7. Match her pace of speech. This builds trust. Then begin to direct the pace of speech. Slow down when you're making a point. Watch to see if she follows you and slows her pace of speech. If she doesn't, you may not have her trust.

8. Look for an invitation to get closer emotionally. If you have done a good job building trust during the discussion, the other person will begin to feel comfortable and will "invite" you into her comfort zone. She exhales, relaxes, sits back in her chair, takes her arms away from her chest, looks you in the eye, and smiles. This signals a readiness to go deeper—a readiness to receive. This is when you can take the conversation to the next level. This part of the process takes patience and creativity as comfort zones fluctuate throughout a conversation.

But be careful. Going deep too fast implies a level of intimacy that you have not yet earned and may kill a deal or raise suspicion of your motives. This erodes trust, and the other person will resist following your lead. However, missing this "invitation" is equally bad. It could be interpreted that you lack confidence. And no one follows an insecure leader.

9. Be okay with uncertainty. If you get pushed out of your comfort zone because you don't know how to respond to a question, you may lose confidence. Stay in neutral. You don't have to have all the answers. Say that you're not sure and ask for her thoughts. Explain that you will do a little research and get back to her. Don't get anxious. This makes you grab at the first solution that arises in the moment. This solution may not be the best. Take your time.

10. Schedule the next step. Schedule a follow-up meeting to check the status of action items. Or, if this is a sales conversation, ask her to buy if she appears ready. She is ready if she has been leaning forward in her chair, smiling, making eye contact, and expressing interest in your work. Her energy should feel positive and eager. If she is not ready, asking for a sale will be premature. Save it for the next encounter.

Knowing how to use comfort zones will get you better results. But the real experts at reading comfort zones are the horses. Here are a few stories from the herd.

What the Horses Say

Courting Cali's Comfort Zone

During an *Alpha Horse Leadership Training for HUMANS*™ workshop, I asked participants one-by-one to go in the ring with Cali and see if they could feel her comfort zone. Cali stood in the arena with her tail facing the group. The first participant, Jack, walked around Cali, stopped about 5 feet away, and stuck his arm out toward her head. His back was straight and he leaned forward toward Cali's face. His feet were firmly planted in the ground. He waited a moment in this position, his eyes focused on hers. She ignored him. He continued to walk around her and try this same approach from different distances. She continued to ignore him. Jack left the arena.

Then Jenny entered the arena. She walked around the arena and stayed about 10 feet away from Cali, her eyes on the ground. Cali stood still and ignored her. Jenny turned her body sideways and walked in a little closer, her eyes averted. She stopped about 6 feet out and extended her hand loosely in Cali's direction, keeping her eyes on the ground and her feet offset. Cali turned her head and looked at Jenny. Jenny stood still. Cali exhaled and closed her eyes. Jenny left the arena.

I asked Jack and Jenny about their experiences. Jack said that he was a little nervous and extended his arm so that Cali could sniff him and get to know him. He watched her face to see her expression, but he didn't feel anything from her. Jenny said that she felt Cali was a little nervous so instead of approaching her from the front, she approached from the side. She avoided eye contact because she thought that would add too much pressure for Cali. Jack said that he was watching for physical responses and didn't seem to get any reaction from the horse. Jenny commented that she felt Cali acknowledged her by looking at her. She said Cali's comfort zone was more energetic than physical and subtle.

This exercise required an awareness of other. In this case, the "other" was Cali. Jack's focus was on his nervousness and on seeing a physical response from Cali. Jenny focused on Cali's comfort and felt an intuitive response. Cali reflected Jack's nervousness and stiff-armed approach by being nervous herself and avoiding eye contact. His physical proximity and approach were too close for her comfort. He had overstepped a boundary. Cali felt more comfortable with Jenny's physical distance and softer approach.

Noble Oversteps?

During another workshop, I used my horse Noble for the comfort zone exercise. The goal was to find Noble's comfort zone. Tina offered to go first.

I opened the gate and Tina entered. Noble stood close to me at the gate. I moved him away using energy to give us some space. He walked backward about 5 feet and stopped. He faced us, his ears pricked, his eyes bright.

As I started to talk with Tina about the exercise, Noble walked up to Tina and sniffed her. She reached out and pet his face, laughing. Then he put his nose in her face and she backed up. I asked her how she felt. She said she was fine; he was just playing. I told her that if he was violating her comfort zone that she could push him away. "No," she said; she was fine. Noble then took her zipper in his mouth and pulled on her jacket. Tina looked at me. I asked her what she wanted to do. She said leave. I said okay. She ran out of the arena. I was surprised. I thought she meant she would move away from Noble to another part of the arena. But Noble had come too close too early, violating her comfort zone and pushing her into flight. Tina was too afraid to stand her ground.

The next participant was Jerry. He walked into the arena, stood up straight, and looked Noble in the eye. Noble backed up and stood still. Jerry walked around Noble. Noble watched Jerry's every move. Then Jerry moved in a bit closer. He was about 4 feet away. His body faced the same direction as Noble's. Jerry took a step. Noble followed. Jerry took another step and Noble continued to follow. They walked all over the ring together, around cones and barrels and over poles. When they stopped, their feet were positioned exactly the same. Noble was quiet and attentive.

After, Jerry told me that he thought Noble was confident, smart, playful, and trusting. He also said that without an equally confident partner, Noble could take over and push someone beyond his or her comfort zone. Jerry directed Noble's energy and interest in an activity. This created a bond. Jerry's confidence and approach established him as a leader. His energy gave Noble a clear boundary, which Noble respected. The horse never once tried to push Jerry beyond his comfort zone. Jerry's awareness of "other" allowed him to assess what Noble needed to follow his lead.

The Color of Footsteps

Melissa, an entrepreneur, brought her horse, Turbo, for a private session on courting prospects and building client relationships. We decided to play with color energy. I asked Melissa to consider the question, "If energy is held in your footsteps and it had a color, what color would it be?" Melissa walked around the ring alone, feeling her energy and focusing on her footsteps. "Brown," she said, and kind of heavy.

"What if you changed them to pink?" I asked. Melissa lifted her body taller, her stride became bouncy, and she took a bigger step. Then she imagined her footsteps as purple and seemed to walk even lighter. She was happiest in purple, she said. She changed the colors back and forth as she walked. Her stride reflected the vibrance of the different colors.

During this time, Turbo ignored her and explored the other side of the arena.

I switched her attention to Turbo. "What color are his footsteps?" I asked. "Brown," she responded. I asked her to walk with him "brown." She walked over to Turbo and he fell in step with her. They traveled around the arena shoulder-to-shoulder without a rope.

I asked her to invite him to walk in another color. She chose pink. Turbo pinned his ears and shook his head, a horse's signs of annoyance. Melissa walked around the course trying to have him join her in pink, but he was quite resistant, even reaching out to bite at one point with his ears back. She said he preferred brown and went back to brown. He settled and walked quietly by her side. The only difference was the color change in Melissa's imagination.

During our debrief, Melissa considered lessons from the exercise for her business. She concluded that you shouldn't make changes too fast with your clients or prospects. If you do, you risk pushing them out of their comfort zone. Turbo was comfortable in brown and resistant to change. Melissa added that you must make changes little by little and gauge their reaction to maintain trust. If they get nervous, go back to where they felt safe. By changing from brown to pink and purple, Melissa's behavior was different from normal, causing Turbo to lose trust and get suspicious. Melissa said that it's important to have a solid relationship before you ask others to follow you into new territory.

Key Points/Questions to Consider

Knowing your comfort zone and identifying the comfort zone of others begins with self-awareness. The better you know yourself, the faster you can make shifts necessary to make others feel comfortable. The more comfort you give others, the more they trust you and will follow you.

The best leaders continue to challenge themselves to learn and grow. They listen to feedback from others, consider new options, and make changes in their approach to optimize success. They are always willing to look at themselves and do things differently.

Observe yourself and your interactions throughout the day. Consider the following questions:

- When are you in your comfort zone?

- How do you know?

- Watch a staff person, a colleague, or client. Is she in her comfort zone?

- What can you do to make her more comfortable?

- Try it. Did it work? How did you feel?

- What else can you do to make them comfortable?

Chapter 7

Secret #5: Recognize Fear and Push Through!

Managing fear is essential to inspired leadership. You must take risks to advance a business and maintain your competitive advantage. And with risk comes fear. Fear of doing the wrong thing, making the wrong decision, losing money, public humiliation. Fear of failure. Fear of success. Yikes!

Even the most confident leader can get stuck in fear. And stay stuck. Unable to move forward. Fear wears many disguises. You may not recognize it. But it holds you back nonetheless.

For example, how many times have you heard someone say, "I'd love to do that, but now is not a good time." Or, "That sounds like a great idea. Let's consider it after we deliver this project." Except that each time the idea is presented, you hear the same response. The "great idea" is put on perpetual hold.

Inspired leaders know that "great ideas" are central to innovation and require careful consideration. Not all are worthy of pursuit. But considering "great ideas" opens your mind to possibilities and opportunities you may not otherwise see. Nurturing "great ideas" breeds a culture of creativity, and your staff feels heard and engaged. It's exciting to work with a leader willing to take risks to bring out the best in the company. Just look at Google; they've done pretty well!

Pursuing that "great idea" requires you to do something different. To look beyond your usual approach and take different action.

To create a new paradigm, break old patterns, and consider various options. You must be more outspoken and visible, reach out to new potential partners, and often invest more capital. This feels uncomfortable and unsafe. And what if it fails? But what if it succeeds?

No one becomes super-successful by playing it safe. You must take risks and face your fear.

The horses have taught me a lot about risk-taking. Physical risk, emotional risk, and financial risk. At times, it wasn't pretty. I've had broken bones, a damaged ego, and lots of debt. Sometimes I even felt like quitting. Especially after one wreck left me unable to work for six months. But I didn't. My passion was too strong.

In this chapter, I'll share techniques for managing fear so you can move forward in confidence. And the horses will offer their wisdom to help you push through resistance and meet your goals. But first, let's take a look at some indicators that fear may be holding you back.

Signs that Fear May Be Holding You Back

When you decide to pursue something new, you step into unknown territory and push yourself to play a bigger game. It can be exhilarating and terrifying at the same time. Believe me, I know!

When I left my director job at a world-class engineering firm to start my current company, I was excited and terrified. I felt the same when I jumped off the corporate track to run a staffing startup. In both cases, I had to think differently, consider new business models, and reinvent myself in this industry space. I had to create a reputation from scratch and prove my worth.

The rejection was painful. In the beginning, I made sales call after call with no success. Some people were nasty and hung up on me. But I finally found my voice. The staffing firm earned $2.1 million in its first year! But the first six months were rough.

Feeling fear during this process is totally normal. To stretch into a new space, you must expand personally and professionally, and take on new challenges. It will be bumpy. Most transitions are.

But there is a difference between feeling uncomfortable because you're stretching into something new and being blocked by fear.

How do you know? Here are seven indicators of how fear may be showing up.

7 Indicators of Fear

1. You procrastinate. Your to-do list is comprehensive, but you're too busy to act on the one thing that will give you the biggest result. This often manifests as the "when I, then I" syndrome. For example: *When* you have $100,000, *then* you'll hire more staff. But the $100,000 gets spent on other things or you never build up this reserve. This also applies to your personal life. *When* I lose 20 pounds, *then* I'll buy that designer suit I've been eyeing. But you never lose 20 pounds. Why not just buy the suit in a bigger size? Why not invest in hiring that staff person to help get you where you want to go?

2. You can't commit. When you make a decision, you often go back on it. Like a turtle shrinking back into its shell, you go back to old familiar patterns and ways of thinking.

3. You worry. A lot. Worry keeps you from living in the *now*— the present. It replays negative experiences from your past and creates images of all the bad stuff that could happen in the future. Worry also prevents you from enjoying past successes; you focus on what you should have done better.

4. You play it safe, but want more. Your business is profitable and you toy with taking it to the next level. But you see expansion as additional pressure and uncertainty. You're scared you may not have what it takes. And you're afraid that you may become a big success, requiring you to play an even bigger game and potentially expose your weaknesses.

5. You haven't fired that employee, or released that toxic client, friend, or relative. Or spouse. The people you surround yourself with reflect your values and your self-respect. They either support you or they exhaust you. No, you can't "fire"

family members, but you can choose how much time you spend with them.

6. You operate in "crisis-management" mode and deal with issues on the fly since you haven't had time to plan a strategy. You're reactive, not proactive. Being proactive requires you to sit down and consider options for the best way to proceed. To be a leader, you must be decisive and commit to a path. Sometimes, it seems easier to react to circumstances than to create your own destiny. But dealing with crisis is not easy and stress takes a toll.

7. You've settled. You think, "I'm pretty successful. I should be happy." I see this a lot with those working in high-paying but lackluster corporate positions. The "golden handcuffs" keep you loyal, promising vacation time, excellent benefits, and retirement income. But your soul is suffering.

Do any of these resonate? If so, fear is preventing you from moving forward. It's keeping you stuck and undercutting your ability to make decisions to advance your goals. Many people tolerate fear for their entire lives either unaware or unwilling to make the changes that will give them great happiness at work and in life.

To control fear, you must first understand it. Let's take a look at what happens when you're scared.

What Happens When You're Scared?

When you're afraid, your body goes into fight-or-flight mode. Fear starts as an emotional response; you're scared. This triggers a physiological response in your body. Hormones like adrenaline and cortisol are released. Your heart beats faster, your breathing quickens, and you get ready to dash off or go into combat.

This fight-or-flight response begins in a part of your brain called the amygdala. The amygdala is consumed with your survival—keeping you safe. And it does a great job. It has worked to help us out of dangerous situations throughout the history of mankind. But, it cannot tell the difference between a real threat and a perceived threat. It prepares regardless.

Once the amygdala kicks in, the thinking part of your brain, the frontal lobe, takes a back seat. You are now in reaction mode. More oxygen goes to your limbs than to your thinking center, where you make decisions. Your thoughts are now controlled by the fear response. You're less rational, and you see fewer options than when you're calm. The bottom line: You can't think straight. You get stuck in a swirl of fear and don't know which way to turn, or you run.

Horses do the same thing. I've seen some run through fences when they are scared. Horses have a tremendous flight instinct. I've had to de-sensitize many to fear. The best approach is to gain their trust under non-stress conditions and then to incrementally add new challenges. Just like with kids. And dogs. Build trust and confidence.

But, you can never be prepared for everything. For example, I was showing my horse Lila at a dressage competition when someone started a chain saw about 300 feet away. Startled, Lila jumped in the air and spun around. She landed and froze, her head high in the air. I could feel her heart pounding. This is never a good sign for the rider! I leaped off just before she let out a huge buck and tried to bolt from the warm-up ring. She continued bucking, prancing, and kicking out with her hind legs while I led her back to the trailer. Lovely.

After she calmed down, I got back on her. She was still on alert, her eyes wide and looking around for danger. I thought about going home. But once we made it into the show ring, she settled and performed a brilliant test. She was able to manage her fear and focus on her job. We won first place!

A flight response is great if you're in real physical danger, but what if it's all in your head?

What if you start to feel scared as you develop your budget or strategic plan for the next several years? Or as you consider a possible joint venture with a powerful firm? Or in response to an opportunity to give a talk overseas? Or to give a talk just down the street? Fear is not rational and doesn't care how big or small the thing is or if it's real or imagined.

To combat fear, you must shift your thoughts out of fight-or-flight, and back into a place where you can make rational decisions. You need to empower the decision-making part of your brain and relax to see options for a new path. If you don't, your perception of the world may be run by your amygdala and you can get locked in fear. You can't make good decisions from a place of fear.

But how? No worries. Here are some approaches to get a handle on fear.

How to Control Your Fear

Dealing with fear is part of being human. We all feel fear, but inspired leaders seem almost fearless. Do they have special powers? No. They just work through it.

The first step in controlling fear is to lengthen the amount of time between your fear thought and your response. The more time that elapses between a stimulus, your fear thought, and a response, the more options you will see. The additional time moves your brain from the amygdala to the rational center and empowers your decision-making.

This takes practice and gets easier over time.

Here are 10 tips that work for me and that I use with my clients.

10 Tips to Control Your Fear

1. Face your fear. Don't run. Acknowledge it. Feel it and allow it to wash over you.

2. Check the time perspective of your fear. Is the fear true now, or is it old fear or future fear? What evidence do you have that it is a threat now?

3. Consider the worst that could happen. Picture the worst possible outcome. What would happen after that? Then what? Keep asking these questions until you get all the way to the

bottom of the fear. What are you assuming? How else could you consider this?

4. Tap into your subconscious. Ask "What part of me is afraid?" Ask to "talk" to that part. Sometimes experiences from your childhood begin to emerge. Experiences that made you feel unsafe. This part screams an alarm of fear deep in your subconscious. Left unheard, it will continue to cry. Ask this part what it needs to feel safe and listen for the response. I have an "inner saboteur" that freaks out when I begin to overcommit. It fears that I will work without breaks, drive myself to exhaustion, and fail to deliver. But if I listen to it and respect it by taking breaks and working at a sustainable pace, it stays quiet.

5. Consider where you have control. What is in your control? What is beyond your control? Let go of anything beyond your control. Make peace with uncertainty. You don't have to know everything!

6. Know your truth and get present. What is true now? Breathe and list the things you are grateful for, your strengths, and your successes so far. Focus on your heart and breath. Feel the pride and love. Use these as anchors. Your truth is always available to you at any moment. Feel it in your heart and use it to anchor you when you're nervous.

7. Visualize new options. Breathe and picture yourself as a success, having achieved your goal, living your greatness. Picture yourself talking to others about your accomplishments. What would you say? What are you doing? Imprint this daily.

8. Look for role models. They show you what is possible.

9. Build confidence. Look for opportunities to address what scares you little by little. Set small goals and commit to meeting them. Have a plan for what you will do if you get scared. Make decisions using your entire body. Ask your head, heart

and gut and listen for the responses (as we talked about in Chapter 3). Your head may need more proof/data, a plan, more time, or contingencies before you take action. Your heart and gut may need more trust. If you do not have agreement between these three areas, give yourself more time to get what you need to feel confident. This helps you build a strong foundation.

10. Get support. Ask experts for help. Good ones can get you over your fear and fast-track your success. In the past, I never hired coaches to help me meet my goals. I thought I should do everything myself. That I was "supposed" to be able to do everything myself. Now I always use a coach. Even to help me complete this book! This is a little secret among top performers of all sorts—business, entertainment, and of course athletics. They all use coaches to raise their game and stay on track.

Remember: Fear helps to keep you safe. But patterns of behavior that have kept you "safe" may no longer work as you move forward. You have to develop new patterns to think and do things differently. It's just part of the process.

Often people get stuck because they project the person they are today into the vision of their goal. They shrink back because they don't have the skills or confidence to perform the activities in their vision. And this may be true. However, who you are now is not who you will be when you meet your goal. You continue to grow and evolve along the way. You develop more skills and confidence and take bigger risks. The "you" in your vision is a more powerful version of who you are today. You just have to start with who you are now.

Your fear becomes smaller and smaller as you allow your best self to emerge. There will always be new challenges as you play a bigger game, but if you follow the 10 tips, you will nip fear early and stay in a place of confidence.

When I address fear with clients and the horses, "stuckness" shows up every time. The horses teach you how to push past this "stuckness" and keep moving forward. Here are a few stories from the herd.

What the Horses Say

Nina Is a Super Hero

Nina had just experienced a heart-wrenching breakup that left her feeling weak, unsupported, and lonely. She felt powerless and uncertain of her identity without her former partner. Even her work was starting to suffer. She called me desperate for relief.

I chose my senior equine instructor Cali to help Nina find peace. We entered the arena and started with deep-breathing exercises to bring Nina's awareness into her body. She identified where she was holding tension and gave herself permission to release it. Then I focused her attention on her heart and then in her gut. This helped to rebalance her energy throughout her body and find the neutral space (as we discussed in Chapter 4). Cali stood in the center of the ring facing away from us. I left the arena.

I asked Nina to walk around and explore Cali's energy. To see how close she could get to Cali before she felt discomfort in herself or the horse. Nina walked slowly, pausing in places. Cali didn't move. Then Nina moved toward Cali's shoulder and stopped about three feet away. Cali still didn't move.

And then time stood still. Cali and Nina stood like a statue. I could barely even see them breathing. I waited outside the arena and said nothing. You could hear a pin drop. I waited and waited. It was a long time and I was starting to get uncomfortable. But I know that the most important thing I can do in these situations is to just hold the space and wait.

Suddenly I felt a shift. Nina reached her hand out toward Cali. Cali turned her nose toward Nina's hand. And tears began to fall down Nina's cheeks. Silent tears. Cali shifted her hind feet and then her front feet, reflecting the movement of energy, but remained in place.

After a few moments, I entered the ring and asked Nina where she was feeling the energy. "In my heart," she said. "I feel Cali's heart in my heart." She said she didn't know what was going on but that it felt powerful and made her cry.

I asked Nina to embrace that power and to imagine herself as powerful as she could be. What would she look like? She giggled between tears, and said a super hero. I asked her to "be" the super hero, to step into that power and bring it into her body. Cali stood close and watched us, her eyes soft, engaged in this new powerful energy.

Then the three of us walked together around the ring enveloped in the new energy. Our steps aligning. Nina recited power mantras: *I am powerful. I am strong.* She breathed deeply. For this exercise, I attached a lead rope to Cali and let Nina hold the rope. To feel the lightness of the lead as we walked together in this energy.

Once the energy felt secure, I dropped away and Nina and Cali continued to walk together in a shared space of power. Each time Nina's confidence began to wane, Cali walked slower and at times even stopped. I asked Nina to feel the resistance in the lead rope when Cali stopped. Then to recommit to her new power and lean forward toward her goal. To push through the resistance and feel the lightness on the other side. The horse's stop reflected Nina's momentary lapse in confidence. A decision to move forward, feel the resistance, and push through was all that was needed to get Cali moving.

During our debrief, Nina said that once she allowed herself to face her fear and not run from it, she moved forward out of the "stuckness." Feeling the love from Cali's heart gave her support and confidence. And by uncovering her inner "super hero," she could see new possibilities for her life. She could feel the energy needed to maintain this vision and the confidence it required to make it a reality.

Amber Gets Real

Fear can grip you at any stage of life. Amber, a successful business owner for over 20 years, sought me out to help her develop a five-year strategic plan. Her company was ready to make some big changes and expand the business. Amber wanted to work through options and was curious how the horses could assist with this endeavor. I chose Cali as her partner.

After entering the arena, I turned Cali loose and Amber and I sat in chairs across from each other. Cali roamed around the space.

I asked Amber about her goals and to describe her overall company vision for five years out. Amber spoke quickly, shifted around in her chair, and avoided my eye contact. She didn't have a clear vision, so I posed a few questions to help her consider options. But Amber rejected each option. She then listed numerous reasons why none of the options we came up with was feasible. This went on for several minutes. During this time, Cali continued to walk at a brisk pace around and around the perimeter of the space. She never once glanced in our direction.

I could feel the spin of uncertainty in Amber growing stronger. And then I asked, "What exactly are you afraid of?" She looked me nervously in the eye and said, "I guess I'm just scared." At that moment, Cali stopped, turned in our direction, and walked up behind Amber. She placed her nose next to Amber's neck and blew softly into her hair. Amber looked at me in surprise.

I asked her what this could mean. Tears welled up in her eyes and she said, "I guess I'm just so afraid of losing my family. I guess Cali could feel that." It was the first time that Amber had been congruent, in alignment in her head, heart, and gut and trusting with me. Cali validated her congruence and supported her vulnerability.

Amber told me that she was afraid that the expansion of her business would impact her time with her family. She felt time was slipping by. Her kids were getting older and beginning to leave home to start their own lives. Amber was unwilling to give up the precious time she had left with them for her business. She felt conflicted, scared, and out of control. And afraid to do the wrong thing.

We walked together with Cali around the space. I questioned her assumptions about what the future could be. Just because you've done something for 20 years doesn't mean you have to keep doing it the same way. Expanding a business is not necessarily just more of the same. It could look different and perform even better.

I asked Amber to think about her preferred lifestyle and design her business expansion around this lifestyle. She began to present new options. Each time Amber offered an option that excited her, Cali reached over and touched Amber's hair with her nose. Amber began to relax. We concluded the session with Amber looking pensive but hopeful.

Two months later she told me that the experience had changed her life. And I did eventually help her with strategic planning. Fear must be removed first before solid plans can emerge.

Luanne Rides a Wave

Fear also hits during big life transitions. Luanne had been a successful professional for over 25 years and was ready for something new. But she was terrified. As a senior manager, she had led many projects with confidence. But she warned me that she was a bit of a perfectionist and scared to take the wrong move. She asked me to help her consider possibilities for the next phase of her career. I chose Cali to help Luanne gain clarity, confidence, and take the first move.

We entered the arena and started deep-breathing exercises to help Luanne get connected to her body and find the neutral space. Luanne mentioned that she wanted to work on her intuition and leading using intention and energy. So, as I had done with Nina, I asked Luanne to explore Cali's energy and notice what may be happening in her own body. Luanne took a deep breath and approached Cali. Cali stood in the middle of the arena.

As Luanne walked toward Cali, Cali moved away. Cali sauntered over to the red exercise ball and pushed it with her nose. It rolled a few feet. Then she walked to a pole on the ground, sniffed it, and walked over it.

I asked Luanne a few questions. Our conversation went something like this:

Me: What do you think of Cali's behavior?
Luanne: She seems curious.

Me: What else?

Luanne: That she wants to play?

Me: What else could that mean?

Luanne: That she wants me to play? Maybe she wants me
              to be playful?

Me: How would you be playful?

Luanne: Engage her?

Luanne again approached Cali. Cali faced away from her standing still. Luanne walked around her, stopping in places. Cali didn't
move and didn't look at Luanne. I asked Luanne a few more questions.

Me: Where are you holding your energy?

Luanne: In my head. I don't know what she wants from
              me.

At that moment Cali exhaled, turned around, and walked over to
me. She buried her head in my chest and stood still.

Me: What do you think of this?

Luanne: I think she wants your guidance. I think she
              wants you to help her teach me.

Me: What would that look like?

Luanne: Maybe we could do an exercise together? You
              and me?

I walked away from Cali and stood next to Luanne. I asked her
to feel my energy. She said my energy felt calm and quiet. Luanne's
energy felt scattered and uncertain to me. I asked her if it would be
okay if I touched her. She said yes. I reminded her to keep breathing
and focus on her heart and gut.

I reached out and touched her arm. Her energy felt electric—
wild. It was shooting off in all directions. I put my hands on her
shoulders and back and patted her to ground some of the energy. She
breathed and relaxed, and her energy began to feel calm.

Then we linked arms and walked together in neutral energy

while Cali watched. Luanne said she felt more focused and clear. Then I said, "We're going to walk toward Cali with the intention of moving her to the right just by pushing our energy in her direction." As we approached Cali, we both exhaled and "blew" energy at her left shoulder. Cali took two steps to the right and stopped. Luanne and I stopped with Cali. I asked Luanne how she felt.

Luanne: Wow. I wasn't even aware of my body. I was just in the moment. It was kind of like being in water.

Me: Yes, you were in the flow. In the flow, you are fully in the present. Your head, heart, and gut energy is aligned with your intention and you just go. It's like riding a wave that you can direct.

We did this several more times. I encouraged Luanne to find the center of the water, like the center of a wave or current where the flow is even and carries you. I told her to stay in the center while we rode the water toward Cali and allow it to push her where we wanted to go.

Cali moved easily away from us each time in the direction we intended. Luanne was awestruck.

On our final attempt, Luanne noticed that Cali stayed still as we moved toward her, but yielded her body a bit to allow the energy to pass. Luanne thought Cali was telling us to stop. That the lesson had been learned and there was no reason to do more. We stopped. Luanne was amazed at the power of intention and energy and said it felt like a breakthrough in her leadership.

Once you set your intention and are in alignment with your goal, things (and people!) can move easily.

Key Points/Questions to Consider

Controlling your fear starts with self-awareness. Observe yourself throughout the day. Consider the following questions:

- What makes you nervous?

- Why?

- What is this telling you?

- How do you manage fear?

- How else could you manage it?

- What would the horses say?

Go ahead—jump in! Don't let your fear hold you back from living the life you deserve.

Chapter 8

Secret #6: Direct with Intention to Meet that Goal

Leadership is about guiding others, and there are a variety of approaches. My approach is to inspire and motivate another to follow. To build trust, respect, and give them an opportunity to share and cultivate their strengths and interests. To build a partnership that endures throughout time.

Another leadership approach is "command and control." Followers are told what to do and expected to do it. This approach centers on obedience and compliance. And it works well in many instances.

But not with mares. If you want a mare to do something, you ask politely. You never force. You provide options and allow her to choose. And you support her choice by riding her the way she prefers. If you do this, she will be loyal for life and give you her best. If you force her, you may have the battle of your life. And she will resent you and not perform well.

I learned this the hard way. I rode many mares and had to develop a number of techniques to meet my goals. One mare didn't like it if you took the reins too early; she would jump up and down in the air in annoyance. Another lost confidence if you didn't take the reins and became spooky and distracted. Yet another would squat down, throw her front legs out, and pound the ground with her little hooves if she didn't want to do something. If you spanked her, it got worse. But once you redirected her attention, she was perfect. Ah, the girls.

They taught me a lot. And they're still teaching me.

So what does this mean for human leadership?

For me, it means that to get the best results from others, you must engage their strengths. Inspire their internal drive and give them a reason to follow. Earn their respect. Allow their voice to be heard. And trust them. The more trust you have, the more you can ask.

Daniel Pink talks about what motivates others in his excellent book *Drive: The Surprising Truth About What Motivates Us.* He found that people are motivated by autonomy, mastery, and purpose. This means that they work best when given the freedom to make decisions, work in an area in which they excel, and feel connected to the goal of the company. I agree.

It's also important to understand the energy dynamic of leading a team. Teams go through stages as they mature. When you first develop a team, or take over a team, there may be a high level of anxiety among members. As you work together over time, this anxiety is replaced by trust and confidence. As a leader, you must be aware of what stage your team is in to provide the right level of guidance to meet your goals. We'll talk about this in a moment.

In this chapter, we'll look at the dynamics of team formation, discuss the 10 steps to inspired leadership, and then see what the horses have to add about leadership. Let's begin with a discussion of the four stages of a team.

The 4 Stages of a Team

To be a great leader, you must understand the dynamics of team-building. Psychologists discovered that teams evolve through four stages: 1) storming, 2) forming, 3) norming, and 4) performing. As a group matures through these stages, it gains trust and confidence. And performs better. Knowing the stage of your team helps you to give them what they need to optimize results. Let's consider each stage.

1. **Storming.** This stage has the lowest level of trust and the highest level of anxiety. Team members are just getting to know each other in this capacity. Some may have worked together

before, but in another way, and in a different role. Other members may be new. Or the team has worked together for a while, but is dealing with a much bigger or different challenge than it has had before. And some team members may have never worked for you. They don't know your standards. This creates uncertainty. Power struggles may break out and personal boundaries may get crossed causing conflict.

At this stage, members are not yet comfortable about what is expected from them or aware of the unique strengths of other members. Each individual has specific concerns. Among other concerns, they may be fearful that they won't make as big a contribution as they desire, that they may be overlooked, that they may do something wrong, or that their reputation will somehow be compromised.

It's up to you as a leader to reassure this team by clarifying roles and responsibilities, and keeping a close eye on their progress. Each individual must be held accountable for her assignments. At this level, your team needs your full attention and support. It is prone to making mistakes, losing confidence, and creating conflict among members.

2. **Forming.** During this stage, the individuals are gaining confidence in their new roles and responsibilities. They are beginning to understand how their specific role contributes to the overall goal. Relationships are beginning to develop and trust is building. But uncertainty still lingers and the team dynamic is not secure. As a leader, you must continue to enforce your standards, keep their focus on the goal, and be visible and available to support them.

3. **Norming.** At this stage, individuals are comfortable with their roles and responsibilities. They understand your standards and expectations. They are beginning to trust the other team members and work is flowing well. As a leader, you

must continue to provide regular meetings to check in on activities and foster a consistent mechanism for feedback.

4. **Performing.** At this stage, your group is confident and its members trust that each is offering his best. They know exactly what is expected and consistently deliver. Team members feel comfortable offering suggestions to make the product or service even better. They listen to each other and trust each other's expertise. As a leader, you must still provide broad oversight and hold regular meetings to stay on track. At this stage, your team is working as a unit. Team members trust you. And you trust them.

Consider the stage of your team. What stage is it in? What signs do you see? What do you need to do to bring out the team's best?

The four stages of a team concept also apply to business development. When you first start out, you're not always sure what to expect. As your business grows, you gain confidence. But just like with teams, anytime you are presented with a new opportunity, you may get nervous and need time to sort out an approach. You may thrash around considering options, similar to the storming phase. Then you settle on an approach and develop a plan, similar to the forming stage. Then you take action and develop a routine. Things start to fall into place, like norming. Finally, you begin to deliver your expertise and products with ease. You are performing.

Now that you know what to watch for in teams, let's talk about how to be an inspired leader. To optimize your success, integrate all of the other secrets we've discussed so far. Start with tapping into your "other 90 percent," to access your full potential (as we discussed in Chapter 3). Then use the steps that follow to get the results you desire.

10 Steps to Inspired Leadership

The inspired leadership process can be broken down into the following 10 steps. However, leadership is not a linear process. For example, you may get through the first few steps, begin taking action, and realize that your plan needs a major overhaul. Or your client changes the requirements mid-way. Or you hire new staff. Each time this happens, go back to the first step and check your energy to be sure that you are not getting too stressed. Your stress will be reflected by others and will compromise your results. Then revisit the next several steps and make revisions. Inspired leadership is a dynamic process, but once you understand the steps, you can meet your goals.

10 Steps to Inspired Leadership

1. Be aware of your energy and the energy of others. Consider the energy you project. Be sure that it is conducive to what you want to achieve. If you are worried, rebalance your energy to find the neutral space (as we discussed in Chapter 4). Do not lead from an energy of fear. Consider who you need to "be" to meet this goal. Put yourself in that energy. For example, do you need to be more focused, disciplined, flexible, decisive, or confident? Pretend that you are that person now. Imagine what it feels like to be that person. Use all of your senses to be that person in your head. How does it feel? This is how you need to start feeling now. Make a commitment. Make the change. If you do not, your goals may suffer.

    Consider the energy of your team. Does it tend to be positive and eager to embrace new challenges? Does it tend to be cautious? An established team may be ready to go, but a less-experienced team or a new team may need time to gain confidence. And individual energies will vary among the people on your team, but all will follow the most powerful energy in the space. Know your team and give it what it needs to perform at its best. For example, some people need more support than others. For those staff people, check in frequently to be sure they stay focused and on task.

2. Identify the goal. Be specific. What are you trying to accomplish? Talk to your client and find out exactly what he wants. Assume nothing.

3. Develop a plan. Consider options to meeting your goal and select the best path. Engage others to help develop the plan—your colleagues, other experts, key staff, and your client (if appropriate).

4. Share the vision. Share your goal and plan with all who will be involved. Include support staff. Watch their responses and listen to their questions. Be sure your vision is clear in your mind. Use your imagination to create a crystal-clear picture of what you want to happen.

5. Identify roles. Assign roles and tell each party what is expected. Be clear and check if they have questions. To make sure you have the right people in the right places, consider the following questions: What are their strengths, preferences, fears? What is their comfort zone? How much can you push them? What do they need from you to be their best? How much direction do they need? What is their experience level?

6. Set your intention. How does it feel in your head, heart, and gut (see Chapter 3)? Do you believe that you can lead this effort? You may feel fear but still hear a "yes, I can do it" from all three places. This is fine. However, if you hear a "no," take a moment to ask yourself what else you need to accomplish this task. Is the deadline too ambitious? Do you need to hire a subcontractor expert? Are your staff in the right roles? As the horses show us, if your intention conflicts with your belief system, you may get stuck and jeopardize your plan. Give this some thought before you move forward. Go back to step 1 and look at your energy. And work on your mindset (as we discussed in Chapter 3).

7. Take action. Start moving forward with your plan.

8. Check in. Be sure to check in with yourself and others to ensure that they are following the plan. Sometimes leaders march off after giving direction and do not realize that the staff has fallen behind. Get feedback from your team and make course corrections to stay on track.

9. Revise your plan. Even the best-laid plans may need revisions. Go back and adjust your plan for anything that impacts scope or timeline. Perhaps the client scaled back the requirements. Changed the date of a deliverable. Or asked for additional support.

10. Meet the goal and celebrate! After you cross the finish line, be sure to celebrate. Take your staff or client out for lunch; have a party. Do something to reward the effort and show your appreciation.

In my *Alpha Horse Leadership Training for HUMANS*™ workshops, groups of participants work together to inspire and motivate a horse to meet a goal. During these workshops, you see the 10-step process in action and evidence of the "four stages of a team." Let's take a look.

What the Horses Say

Where Are We Going?

During a workshop, I asked a group of four participants to guide my horse Lila around an obstacle course using only their intention, energy, and body language. No rope. The obstacle course included orange cones, two blue barrels, a red ball, and poles on the ground. The goal was to move around the course in a specific pattern and finish by walking together over a pole. They were not allowed to touch Lila.

The participants gathered together to discuss their approach. Lila stood close by. The team established roles: One would be the leader and stay in front, two would walk by Lila's side, and the fourth would follow behind to ensure that Lila stayed on course. Happy with this plan, they walked around Lila to position her in the middle of their group. They began to walk. Lila followed. For about five strides.

Then Lila drifted off to explore something in the corner of the ring. The leader kept walking, head down, focused on staying the course. The other participants walked over to the corner to see what had grabbed Lila's attention. But she was done with the corner.

Lila sauntered over to the window, looked out, and whinnied. The leader stopped walking and started to make her way to the window. The other three participants stared out the window with Lila. The leader glanced out the window. Then they all stood together at the window contemplating their next move.

The leader suggested that they regroup in their original positions and stay closer to Lila to keep her attention on the task. With a bit of hand waving from the person behind, the group marched off again with Lila in the middle. Lila began to drift to one side and the person on that side threw up her arms. Lila moved back into her position.

Then the leader stopped, confused about which way to go next. Lila stopped, too. Then she walked away from the group while they considered which way to go. Lila sniffed the cones and ambled around the arena while the group conferred. They eventually decided to start over and resumed their positions around Lila. With a bit of vocal encouragement from the person behind and the two by her side, Lila began to walk.

The group closed in a bit closer this time as they negotiated the course, circling the barrels and heading for the final ground pole. As they made their way toward the finish line, their footsteps became synchronized with Lila's. Like a marching band in step. They crossed over the pole victorious, smiling and laughing—Lila in the middle of the happy grins.

During the debrief, the participants said how important it was to have a clear vision of what was expected. And they had to be certain that everyone knew their job, and to check in with each other to be sure that everyone was on track.

They also mentioned that it was important to know what Lila needed from them to keep her in line. One participant said that Lila needed more guidance than they had expected. The first few strides had been easy. The leader commented that everything had seemed so easy at the start that she had assumed the rest of the course would be the same. Another participant said that when the leader got confused about the path, the entire group fell apart and Lila drifted off to do her own thing. They mentioned how fast confidence can erode when a leader gets confused.

Another participant commented that they had allowed Lila to draw their attention away from their task and toward what she wanted to do. But, they took the feedback that Lila had provided from the first attempt and changed their approach to be successful on the next attempt.

They also said that at times, they needed a little more energy to keep Lila inspired to stay with them and more support from each other to keep her focused around the course. They also said that Lila was a very willing partner and seemed quite happy to oblige when the direction was clear.

Did you spot evidence of the four developmental stages of a team: storming, forming, norming, and performing? Like people, horses have very different personalities, and what is need to inspire and motivate one may not work for another. And group dynamics can break or make your success. Here's a little story about a group exercise with Cali.

Cali Won't Budge

During another workshop, a group of five participants worked with Cali to perform an exercise similar to the one described with Lila. The goal was to navigate an obstacle course together and cross the finish line, a pole on the ground. Again, the participants were not allowed to touch the horse nor use a rope. They had 20 minutes to accomplish this task.

The group stood together and strategized. Cali stood on the other side of the arena and watched.

The group agreed that first they had to get Cali's attention. One participant rolled a ball at Cali. The ball rolled past Cali. Cali didn't move. Another picked up a cone and waved it in the air. Cali looked at the cone, her ears pricked forward with interest. But she didn't move. Another participant bounced the ball and made kissing sounds at Cali. Cali wouldn't budge.

The group decided that a new strategy was needed. They formed a group around Cali, one person in the lead, two on each side. The persons on the side waved their arms and moved toward Cali, and she started walking. The person at the front looked back to see what was going on then turned around to lead the team. The group moved forward in unison for about three strides. Then Cali stopped, sniffed the ground, and turned her butt toward the group. She marched off in the opposite direction.

The participants scrambled around, calling out to each other to resume their positions and get Cali to turn around. One participant walked off to get a cone. Another stopped and watched. The remaining three walked around Cali to entice her to change direction to no avail. The participants decided that they needed to regroup and rethink their approach. All five moved to the corner of the arena to create a new plan. Cali stood alone on the other side of the arena.

The new plan involved surrounding Cali a little closer, clucking at her, and waving their arms when she deviated from the path. They positioned themselves around Cali and started again. This time Cali walked forward for several strides. Then she stopped, turned left, ignored the arm waving from the person on the left, and walked past her across the arena. The group ran around Cali to find their positions and get her back on track. But when they regrouped, the leader wasn't sure which way to go since now they were facing a new direction. They stopped for a moment and Cali stopped, too. After a minute of discussion, Cali walked away from the group. The time expired. The group was devastated.

During the debrief, some participants voiced how frustrating the exercise had been and that they hadn't been clear on which way they were going before they started. A couple said they felt like failures and that the exercise brought up feelings of insecurity and not being heard. All agreed that Cali was a challenge and they needed more time with each other to figure out how to best work together. One said she never felt that they were a real team. She noticed that each time they strategized, Cali was on the "outside" and should have been considered a team member. Another mentioned that it seemed that they didn't know what to do with the feedback Cali gave them on their approach to successfully meet the goal. Another noted that it was interesting how some folks were taking things so personally and that it was just an exercise that provoked some interesting insights into group dynamics.

Later, the group conducted more exercises to explore these feelings with Lila. They were able to take the teachings from Cali, apply them to Lila, and get very different results. All claimed how easy it was with Lila.

Again, did you find evidence of the four developmental stages of a team in this example: storming, forming, norming, and performing? It's not a linear process. Sometimes teams go back and forth between storming and forming many times before they start to normalize and perform. Did you notice the energy of the participants at the end? How would this energy factor into their results?

The next story is from a private session.

My Head Is Spinning!

Trisha, a retired executive and top-notch horsewoman, called me for a session to explore how equine-assisted coaching could strengthen relationship-building. She was doing volunteer work and was experiencing conflict with an employee. I chose my horse Noble as her partner.

We started with some breathing exercises to find the neutral space and rebalance her energy (as we discussed in Chapter 4). Then I set up a small obstacle course. The goal was to inspire Noble to move around the course without touching him or using a rope. To finish the course, he had to walk between two cones. I left the arena.

Trisha and Noble looked at each other. Then the red ball caught his eye, and Noble trotted over and pushed it with his nose. He struck at it with his front legs, making it bounce and spin. He turned to look at Trisha. She stood in the center of the arena watching. Then she raised her arms and looked to the left. Noble walked to the left.

She walked behind him toward the first element of the obstacle course. He stopped, spun around, and walked in the other direction. She followed him waving her arms slightly to the right. He turned right.

She walked behind him toward another obstacle. In front of the obstacle, Noble spun around to the left and trotted off. Trisha jogged over to redirect him to the right, her hands open, palms out. Noble dodged past her and trotted to the other end of the space. He stopped and looked at her.

She stopped, too. He was about 20 feet away. They stared each other square in the eyes for what seemed like forever, but it was probably a minute. Then Noble leaped in the air and spun around and around, his hind legs kicking out. He landed almost in the same place. He stared directly into Trisha's eyes, shook his head, and stood still. She just stared at him.

I asked her what was going on. She said, "I don't know. I just have so much stuff spinning around and around in my head. I don't know what path to take." I asked her where her energy was. She said her head.

Noble stood quietly. He had not moved since his spinning antics. I reminded her that the horse reflects your emotional state. She chuckled and said she was all spun up in her head. I suggested that she rebalance her energy through her heart and gut. Then reset her intention for what she was trying to accomplish.

Noble waited quietly at a standstill. She took a deep breath, exhaled, stood up straighter, and looked at Noble. He lowered his head and followed her easily through the obstacle course and through the finish line.

During the debrief, Trisha stated that Noble made it quite clear that her direction was not clear. And that her head energy had taken over, preventing her from meeting her goals. She mentioned that at one point during the exercise, she had lost her intention as well as the goal of the activity. But, once she rebalanced her energy and was clear on the objective, the horse was happy to oblige. She said that she'll be sure to rebalance her energy before her next encounter with the employee of concern.

Key Points/Questions to Consider

- To be an inspired leader takes awareness of the energy you carry as well as awareness of others. What is the energy of your team? Does it reflect your energy?

- Consider the stage of your team or business. What stage is it in? What signs do you see? What do you need to do to bring out its best?

- What is your intention today?

- Who do you need to check in with today? Have you checked in with yourself?

Chapter 9

Secret #7: Know When to Stop! Conquer Perfectionism

K nowing when to *stop* is critical to success in life. And inspired leaders know this well. They know how to pace themselves for the long term and avoid burnout.

However, many people are overachievers and have a hard time saying no. They work late into the night and often on weekends. They hold high expectations and drive themselves with intensity.

Some are also perfectionists, people-pleasers, and conflict-averse. They go above and beyond basic requirements. They volunteer in community and business groups. But nothing ever seems to be "good enough," and there is always more to do. They avoid giving themselves a break, afraid they may miss something. This relentless feeling of always needing to do more can begin to damage their health, work, and relationships.

Does this sound familiar?

As a recovering "Type A," I know this firsthand. In my quest to optimize my own potential and deliver my best, I often push myself with rigor. And if I'm not paying attention, sometimes I still try to sabotage my own success. I find myself working without breaks, eating on the run, and indulging my carbohydrate sweet tooth. Left uncontrolled, this makes me tired and fat and unable to deliver my best!

Luckily I've learned to recognize my behavior and rein it in (pardon the pun!). The horses also helped me know when to stop. For example, if you push a horse too hard in training, it may become resentful, refuse to perform, and be really hard to catch from the field the next time. With horses, you must stop while they are still happy and willing to offer their best. If you do this, they will trust you and follow your lead.

People are no different. Like horses, they may get resentful and "hard to catch" if you overwhelm them or push them beyond their limits. Your staff may not be inclined to work as hard. Your prospects may not buy from you if you are too aggressive in a sales pitch or if you overload them with information. At a minimum, they will be cautious.

This also applies to you. You may get resentful that you're driving yourself so hard and feel overwhelmed. You may lose trust in yourself. To know when to stop, you must first look at how you treat yourself. And you must begin to give yourself what you need. In this chapter, we'll outline approaches to help you manage your drive, stay in your place of power, and actually be more productive and more happy. Really. And I'll share more about how the horses help to teach you to stop.

But first, let's take a look at perfectionism and how inspired leaders manage their drive.

Your Perfectionism Is Bad for Your Work!

A strong drive to do things well and be at the top of your game is admirable. The best leaders in the world all have it. It's essential to success in business. However, this powerful drive taken to the extreme can be a killer. It can kill relationships and businesses, and damage your health. How many times have you heard that someone is "married" to their job? Or perhaps you know someone with high blood pressure or chronic back pain from long days at the office? These cases are often the result of not knowing when to stop.

In contrast, inspired leaders know when to stop. They set clear boundaries, expectations, and timelines. They are decisive, deliver on time, empower others, and know when to take the pressure off. They respect and trust themselves and others, and they celebrate success. They maintain their physical, mental, and spiritual well-being to ensure that they can give themselves fully to any task they undertake. They maximize their potential and build a strong foundation for the long term. And they always deliver their best.

But what they deliver is not always perfect. Even the best companies in the world make mistakes. Like Apple or Microsoft when they issue updates to software that was released with a few bugs. The leaders know that making the software available is more important than holding it back because of a little bug. Although this is bothersome to the customer, the bother is temporary. The customers trust that a timely fix will be provided, and it is. The confidence the customer has in the company overrides the blip in the company's performance.

Inspired leaders understand that confidence is a key ingredient to success and they trust themselves to make good decisions. They know what new opportunities to pursue, and just how much to push themselves and their staff to reach goals. They know precisely who they serve. And they also know when to say no; they don't accept all clients, or pursue all projects, or attend all meetings or trade shows. They know exactly where they should be and what they should be doing to achieve their objectives. And, they know how to negotiate reasonable deadlines to keep clients happy.

Does this sound like you? If not, you may need to stop. You may need to consider new options for how you work. Let's take a look at a few signs that you may need to take a break.

Signs that You May Need to Stop

Not knowing when to stop and perfectionism both originate from fear. You fear that if you stop and take a break, something will fall apart. That you will lose control. But the reality is that you've already lost control. Just take a look at your to-do list for today. Can you really get all of that done in one day?

Let's pause for a moment. Yes, stop. Take a breath. And another. It's time to get really clear on how you're running your life. Here are some signs that you may need to stop and make a few changes:

1. You're exhausted.
2. You're unsure and avoid making decisions.
3. You're profits could be greater.

Let's look at these three more closely.

You're Exhausted

In giving yourself to your work and others, you sacrifice your own needs. You drink cup after cup of coffee. You miss your workouts. And put your vacation plans on hold. You fall into bed at night dead tired. And then its morning and it starts all over.

Subconsciously you may believe that everyone else is more important than you. Your "busy-ness" becomes an indicator of your self-worth. Your subconscious believes that "if I'm really busy all the time, I must be valuable." You seek external validation to fill a void deep inside yourself. You fill this void with work.

But saying yes to working more is not the answer. Once you become known as a "yes man" (or "yes woman") you set a pattern of expectation. Others expect you to always be available. An endless stream of tasks builds up on your desk. It's ironic: You fear if you do not say yes, you may lose everything you worked so hard to create. But by saying yes to everyone except yourself, you're exhausted and unable to keep up. You have no boundaries, and others seem to lack respect for your time. But they are only mirroring your own lack of respect for your time.

You're Unsure and Have Trouble Making Decisions

All activities on your to-do list seem critical and some may seem impossible to complete on time. And the list gets longer every day. You're not sure how or if you'll get it all done.

Your uncertainty is reflected in your staff's performance. If you are driving at too fast a pace and not entirely sure how to proceed, mistakes are inevitable and you must backtrack. This eats up valuable time, creates more stress, and causes your staff to lose confidence. And, if you say yes every time a client changes his mind without renegotiating an appropriate timeline, you'll add more stress. The pace is not sustainable without a break, and some staff may burn out and leave. If you don't have staff, this all applies to you alone.

Your Profits Could Be Greater

You know you should take your firm to the next level, to maximize its potential. Or, that you should seek that promotion. But you're so busy managing your current workload that it seems impossible to do right now. And you're uncertain of the next step. You may also be so preoccupied with your current workload that you don't recognize a potential opportunity. A "yes" to this new opportunity would advance your goals. But, the prospect feels your lack of focus as a lack of interest and backs away. You're leaving profits on the table.

Or, you are not charging what you are worth. Your current clients are not the highest-paying ones, but the income is steady. You fear that increasing your rates may drive them away. So you tolerate their demands. But, you are so busy with them that you are unable to court new prospects that could give you better opportunities and pay you what you're worth.

Finally, if you delay a product launch or delivery because of your perfectionism, you will lose money. In many cases, companies cannot invoice until a delivery is made. The longer you delay a delivery, the more you impact your cash flow. In addition, time that you spend holding that product could be used to develop a product that will attract high-paying clients.

Do you recognize any of these signs? Any can sabotage your success. All cause stress and exhaustion. They also make you do even more to try to keep up. It's a vicious circle and unsustainable.

The truth is that when you take breaks, give yourself and staff time off, and set clear boundaries, you actually get more done! This is a key part of setting yourself up for sustainable long-term success. Let's explore how to *stop* and then look at how horses teach us this valuable secret.

How to Stop

The most important key to knowing how to stop is to listen to yourself. To be more self-aware and conscious of your beliefs and actions. Once you are aware, you can begin to question limiting beliefs and make shifts to allow more success.

For example, feel the difference in energy that excites and motivates you to be your best versus energy that causes too much pressure. There is a fine line. But both rely on adrenaline. The best leaders know how to use the right amount of adrenaline to inspire results. But too much adrenaline over time causes stress and is not sustainable.

The best way to use adrenaline is to put pressure on for short, focused spurts and then take the pressure off. Stop before you get exhausted. And celebrate small successes. Appreciating the small stuff sets a vibration of positivity that elevates your mood, allows you to revel in your accomplishments, and inspires you and your team to keep going.

Let's look a bit more at energy.

Consider the energy that drives you. Is it based on beliefs of abundance or lack? If you are driven by beliefs based on abundance, you are excited to share your products and services. You know your value and how much you help others. You believe that there are many potential clients that will purchase from you.

In contrast, if you are driven by beliefs based on lack, you are also excited to share your products and services, but you are afraid that the client you have now may be the only client you ever get! You believe that there is a limited pool of prospects and that your competition may get to them first.

Can you feel the difference in these energies? Knowing the energy of your drive helps you to understand why you do the things you do. The great news is that once you are aware, you can make changes to improve. And you can start now.

By the way, I have never known a leader that has been able to drive nonstop. Something will make you stop if you don't do it yourself. Burnout and health-related issues are rampant among perfectionists.

So, here are a few practical tips to help you stop undesired behavior, be more productive in less time, and get happier! Don't feel like you have to do everything on this list (I know you overachievers!). Just pick one or two that resonate and start with those. Or find something else that works for you.

10 Tips to Stop and Conquer Perfectionism

1. Identify your personal needs and set boundaries. What sustains you? What makes you feel great? Create a daily routine to give yourself what you need. Build in time to recharge every day. Schedule this time and honor it as you would any client agreement. This practice helps set you up for success. Set aside time each day—even just 20 minutes of quiet meditation, exercise, or anything that makes you happy—as your special time. I encourage my clients to do this in the morning to avoid competing with other priority activities later in the day. Get up a little earlier if you have to; it will be worth it. I take walks in nature most days. It sustains me and I notice when I miss a day. And set boundaries on your work hours and e-mail availability. Unless you're on call 24 hours a day, you don't need to be available all the time.

2. Set goals. Set business goals and personal goals. Setting goals
    helps you reconnect with why you're doing what you're do-
    ing. What do you want for your business or work in the next
    year or longer? What do you want it to look like three to five
    years out? Do the same for your personal life. This is how you
    begin to live by your own design. And check in with your
    goals; they can change over time. Stay in touch with what
    you really want.

3. Be decisive. Review your to-do list and determine what ab-
    solutely must get done that day. Also consider if something
    has to get done at all. Identify the activities that have the
    biggest impact—the ones that will advance progress toward
    your goals. Be sure to take action daily on these priorities.
    Everything else can wait or be delegated. And make sure the
    daily tasks are doable in that day. Don't over-reach. If you set
    out to do more than is possible, you set yourself up for failure
    and perpetuate your overwhelm. Use your head, heart, and
    gut to help you make decisions on priorities (as we discussed
    in Chapter 3).

4. Stay in your place of power. Do what you do *best* and out-
    source the rest. Work where you have the most impact and
    add the most value. This is your place of greatness. Identify
    and honor your specific core talents and strengths, and give
    them what they need to flourish. Allow them to be seen and
    heard. Look for ways to showcase them (e.g., public speak-
    ing, writing articles, and conducting radio and television in-
    terviews). Say no to anything outside of your place of power.
    By delegating to others, you empower them to be their best.
    Don't try to do everything yourself; hire staff, subcontractors,
    and consultants to support you.

5. Listen to others. Give them your full attention. In striving
    to meet goals, perfectionists can get "tunnel vision" and only
    see and hear what they want to see and hear. Tunnel vision

can be blinding, and you may miss important details and opportunities. You may even miss when a prospect says yes to your offer if you are pushing too hard. Listen carefully and assume nothing. In all conversations, you must be fully present to quickly adjust your approach based on feedback you're getting from the other party. If you are pushing a specific agenda, you may not be able to listen.

6. Know when you have "enough" content. Perfectionists and overachievers like to share everything they know. But what works best is to keep things simple. As simple as possible. And relevant. Figure out what someone wants and needs. And give it to her. Do not overwhelm her with detail. Always think from your client's perspective and your staff's perspective: What is the most critical thing they need to hear or see or do? Address those points. And only those points. This applies to everything from conducting meetings, teaching, giving presentations, to developing software. You must know when it's time to stop or risk losing your audience, running out of money chasing down details, and developing something too complicated. And not what they wanted.

7. Deliver on time. Make every attempt to bring your best to your client. But don't hold off on delivery due to perfectionism. If you anticipate that a deadline is too ambitious, negotiate a new date. But if you fear delivering something because it's not absolutely perfect and you keep delaying the due date, the client will begin to lose trust. Talk with the client about options; deliver a working draft or part of the project. Communication builds trust. Offer the client version one with an update the following week. Don't box yourself in, and don't make a client wait. Her expectations only get higher while her trust in you erodes if she doesn't see something. If you do deliver an interim product, be sure it's a strong indication of the quality to come and that your client knows it is not final.

8. Be sure your values are expressed in your life. At work and outside of work. These are the things that sustain you. They give you energy and make you happy. If your values are repressed, you may have a values conflict; you may be driving yourself to exhaustion for something you don't even value and avoiding the thing that will give you the most joy. For example, if you say you value good health, but you never work out and you always eat on the run, you have a values conflict. Make some changes if this is the case. Take control of your life.

9. Take frequent breaks throughout the day. And schedule vacations. To maximize your potential, use your entire body. If you have been working at the computer, take a short walk break or get up and stretch every hour. If you have been silent, go talk to someone. If you have been with many other people, be silent for a while. Switch up the mental and physical focus throughout the day to keep yourself fresh and avoid exhausting one part of your body. It's usually the brain that gets overworked. Give it a brief rest.

10. Celebrate your success! Be proud of everything that you have done. No success is too small. Reward yourself. Go out with friends. Take a trip. Buy that outfit you've been eyeing. Heck, take a nap! Or do nothing.

Once you begin to implement these tips, they will start to become habits, and you will get more done in less time and feel happier. You actually become more productive by allowing your drive to run unencumbered by fear.

Now let's explore what the horses have to share on this topic. They are quite clear on how to stop and listen for a yes. They also show you what can happen when you keep pushing.

What the Horses Say

"Yes" Can Be Very Quiet

Dana came to me to refine her prospecting and sales conversations and close more deals. We narrowed her target market to retired women. Then she partnered with her horse, Luke, to simulate the prospect courting process. In this scenario, Luke the horse played the role of her prospect, a retired woman.

After entering the arena with Dana and Luke, I asked Dana a few questions:

Me: What energy do you need to court your prospect?
Dana: Gentle, open energy.
Me: What is the first thing you'll do to develop a relationship?
Dana: Just walk with him to get to know him.

She followed Luke as he traveled around the arena and then she walked by his side. They fell in step shoulder-to-shoulder and walked together for several minutes. All of the work was done without a lead rope or any attachment to the horse. Luke's head was low and he followed Dana's every move.

Next, Dana designed an exercise to advance the relationship and courting process. She decided that a specific simple task would be a good next step. She put two poles on the ground about 10 feet apart; the goal was to walk with Luke around the arena at her side, then walk between the poles together, and finish by stopping together on the other side. Achieving this goal would mean that she effectively completed a "sale" and gained a new client.

On the first attempt, Dana stood by Luke's side and took a step. Luke followed her for a couple of steps and then walked in the opposite direction. He wandered all over the arena sniffing the ground, exploring. At times he joined Dana's side but then drifted off to sniff other parts of the arena. Dana stood in one spot and watched, contemplating whether to redirect his attention. Luke ambled over to the poles and walked through by himself. Dana said, "Good boy," and he stopped and faced her on the other side, his head lowered and licking his lips.

Dana immediately walked up to Luke and put her hand briefly on his head to guide him back toward the poles to finish the exercise together in the "right" spot. But he moved away from her, his ears slightly back, his tail swishing—a horse's signs of displeasure. He traveled around the arena alone. Dana stood and watched for a moment. Then she walked toward his shoulder and they walked side-by-side around the space. At times, he drifted from her side and she followed him a few steps before he fell back in stride with her at her side.

She guided him toward the poles again to complete the exercise. In front of the poles, Luke stopped dead in his tracks. Dana continued through the poles and stopped on the other side. Luke watched her. His eyes stared straight into hers for a minute. Then she called his name. He exhaled and walked slowly through the poles. She said "ho" softly, and he stopped near the place she had selected as the finish line.

From this exercise, Dana concluded that retired women need to be allowed to "drift," make their own decisions, and be guided gently through the sales process. She said she felt like she could easily lose the connection with Luke if she rushed the process or used more force. She said it was better to encourage Luke to follow her but also allow him to explore. She said she stopped and watched him a couple times during the exercise to see what he would do and gather information to help her develop the relationship. She said she used her voice at the end since he seemed to need more incentive to follow her. He needed just a slight push, she said, but nothing too forceful.

I then asked Dana a few questions about the first attempt with Luke when he wandered through the poles on his own. Our conversation went something like this:

Me: What was his body position? How did he seem to
        feel after this first attempt?

Dana: He seemed relaxed, like he felt safe. He was yawning and licking and chewing. His head was lowered.

Me: Did he seem happy?

Dana: Yes.

Me: Did he do the exercise?

Dana: Maybe, but he didn't really do it because I asked him. It was kind of random, and he didn't stop in the place I marked as the finish line.

Me: What was his reaction when you touched his head to guide him back to the poles?

Dana: He put his ears back. He seemed angry and moved away from me.

Me: What could that mean?

Dana: That he didn't like me touching him?

Me: What else?

Dana: [laughing] That he had completed the exercise the first time and didn't want to do it again.

Me: How did he behave after this first attempt?

Dana: He didn't seem to want to follow me as easily and I had to gain his trust all over again. And it took longer.

Me: What could this mean for your prospecting?

Dana: That I need to watch more closely for a soft yes and stop selling at that point. Otherwise I might lose them.

Me: What else?

Dana: That you don't have to sell the entire package on a first date.

Me: What else?

Dana: That I'm a perfectionist! I wanted to finish at the exact place I marked. I have to be okay with accepting "good enough."

Dana also commented that a "sale" may not look like what you intended. She noticed that her desire to do the exercise perfectly clouded her ability to recognize an early yes from her horse. Her need for perfection compromised the trust she had built during their first walk around the arena and almost ruined the sale.

New Roles Emerge

A mother and her daughter were having an identity crisis. They loved each other deeply, but their roles were shifting and it was affecting their relationship. The daughter was now an adult and living on her own. They came out to strengthen their communication skills and explore new ways of relating as adults. I selected my horse Cali as their partner.

We started outside of the arena with some breathing exercises to get calm and centered, and find the "neutral space" (see Chapter 4). Then I asked them to walk with Cali through a small obstacle course without using a lead rope. Cali was drawn to their energy and sniffed their hair, hands, and bodies. She stood close to their sides. Cali seemed especially interested in the mother and licked her hands. Before embarking on the exercise, the pair discussed their approach and decided to use Cali's interest in the mother as enticement. The daughter suggested that her mother stay in the middle and hold her hands out to Cali. The daughter would lead the three of them around the course. It worked.

They walked together slowly and deliberately around the arena, over poles on the ground, and between barrels and cones. A couple of times Cali started to drift, but the daughter quickly noticed and told her mother exactly where to move to regain Cali's attention. The mother followed her suggestions without question. At one point Cali stopped and refused to move. Both mother and daughter stopped and waited. All three stood in silence. Then the mother offered her hands to Cali. After a moment, Cali exhaled, turned, and followed her. The daughter resumed her position at the front and they completed the task.

We made the next exercise a bit more challenging. They had to walk together through a complex obstacle course with more twists and turns while rolling an exercise ball. To finish, they had to get Cali to walk backward into a "parking space" designated by two poles on the ground.

They started off using the same approach as before with the mother in the middle. The daughter rolled the exercise ball as she led them around the course. As they neared the end, Cali stopped dead right outside the parking space, the finish line. The mother and daughter discussed their options, and one went on one side of Cali and the other walked to the opposite side. Cali didn't move for a few seconds and then she walked off away from the poles. Both mother and daughter watched. Cali stopped again about 15 feet away. The mother started to move toward Cali, but her daughter said no. They waited. Finally Cali turned toward them and walked up to them. The three stood together, and the mother and daughter looked at me. I asked them a few questions. Our conversation went something like this:

Me:	How are you feeling in your head, heart, and gut?
Mother:	I'm not sure what to do.
Daughter:	Me either.
Daughter:	She seems confused.
Me:	Are you confused?
Daughter:	Yes. I'm just not sure of the best way to get her in the parking space.
Me:	What were you feeling when you had her near the parking space with each of you next to her side?
Daughter:	Like she had too much pressure. That's why she walked away.
Me:	I noticed that you told your mom not to follow her. Why?
Daughter:	Because Cali was feeling too much pressure. She needed space.

Me:	So you stopped doing something.
Daughter:	Yes. I wanted her to be able to come back and trust us.
Me:	And what happened?
Daughter:	She came back.

Yes. Cali returned to them after they released the pressure. At the end of the obstacle course, both mother and daughter felt pressure to complete the task but didn't know exactly how to get Cali into the parking space. Their energy and emotions caused Cali to move away. She was reflecting their emotional state. When they took the pressure off by stopping and giving her space, Cali came back. They allowed Cali the freedom to make her own decision.

We discussed parallels to their own relationship, and the mother mentioned that their shifting roles were mirrored in their work with Cali. With the horse, the mother allowed her daughter to take the lead and trusted her judgment. The mother mentioned that she always wants to fix everything for her daughter and has trouble allowing her to make her own decisions. This creates pressure and sometimes causes problems in their relationship.

Both mother and daughter recognized the need to stop pushing, stop trying to fix things, and stop trying to make everything perfect. They saw the value in taking the pressure off of Cali and the reward of her trust. They also acknowledged that even though they did not get Cali in the parking space, it was more valuable to stop in a place where the trust was high instead of risking ruining the trust that they had gained by working together.

Sometimes it's best to stop. Inspired leaders never chase. They create an environment that fosters trust and openness. The goal of this session was relationship-building, not making a horse move into a certain place.

Sometimes you can get so focused on what you're *not* doing well that you can't see what you *have* accomplished. Refocus the lens and see all the greatness that you have achieved. No matter how small!

Key Points/Questions to Consider

Knowing when to stop starts with self-awareness. Take a moment to consider the following questions when you begin to feel stressed. Your responses will help you regain your balance and make decisions in your own best interests.

- What is my goal? At work? In life?

- Consider the next item on your to-do list. Will this take me closer to my goal?

- Will this activity nourish me and give me energy, or will it drain my energy?

- What is my body telling me about this activity/opportunity/ person? How does it feel in my head, heart, gut?

- What would happen if I took this out of my life? What else? So what?

- Why will I not stop? What am I afraid of? What am I running from?

- What am I missing in my life? Why am I not satisfied?

- What am I running to?

- Am I present?

- What would be gained by stopping?

- What am I assuming? Is this true?

- How else can I think about this?

Conclusion

Now you know the secrets to inspired leadership. And how horses can show you the way.

We began our journey together with the question, "How do you inspire and motivate another to follow your lead?" As the horses have demonstrated, inspired leadership starts with you. Your energy. Your intention. Your mindset.

So, tap into your "other 90 percent" and lead with conviction. Keep your emotional balance by finding neutral. Trust yourself and others. Use your head, heart, and gut to make great decisions. Radiate confidence and positivity to draw others to you.

Be respectful of comfort zones. Push through your fears. Don't let anything hold you back.

The growth of a business depends on the growth of its leaders. Their willingness to take chances, step into fear, and believe in themselves, their people, and their work. So claim your place of power and be the leader you know you can be. You deserve to live your life on your own terms.

And know when to take a break. When to stop. And celebrate your success no matter how small.

Now it's time to take what you've learned and lead with vigor. You have a unique gift that you and only you can offer. Use these secrets to get out there and share it!

Remember the three things that I know for sure:

- You can create something out of "nothing."

- You can make money doing what you love.

- At any point, you can reinvent yourself.

With passion and a little creativity, anything is possible.

Thank you so much for staying with me throughout this book. I hope you find these secrets helpful. They have taken me a lifetime to learn and lots of bumps and bruises. And the horses have more to teach. Hopefully without the bumps and bruises!

I wish you the best of success. Here's to your inspired leadership!

Shari Jaeger Goodwin

For More Information

For more information on Shari's programs, go to www.jaeger2. com. From this site, you can sign-up to receive a FREE guide, *7 Steps to Make More Money in Business*, and get success tips from Shari and the horses.

Also join us on social media:
Facebook: facebook.com/ShariJaegerGoodwin
Twitter: twitter.com/ShariJGoodwin

Shari has numerous programs available to help you raise your game and achieve your goals. Contact us at www.jaeger2.com for information on private coaching, customized group programs and training, and speaking events. We'd love to help you. Here's to living your greatness!

About the Author

Shari Jaeger Goodwin is a business strategist, leadership coach, speaker, and trainer. She blends her love of the natural world with proven techniques to raise your game, achieve your goals, and live happy and fulfilled. Animals have always played a huge role in her life. After graduating from college with dual degrees in zoology and English, friends and family jokingly compared her to "Dr. Doolittle." Her love of natural systems drove her to pursue a Master's degree in biology with a focus in environmental science. She also has a strong music background and played clarinet and saxophone in numerous bands in her early years including jazz bands, orchestras, symphonies, and theatre groups.

Shari is an avid researcher and writer and is always looking for new ways to inspire peace and joy while achieving goals. This drive prompted the creation of her unique leadership model which she teaches in her signature *Alpha Horse Leadership Training for HUMANS*™ workshops. These workshops have been called "profound" and "life-changing." Her leadership model centers on emotional intelligence and has been hugely effective in teaching sales.

Shari explores life with an open mind and a sense of humor and takes great joy in the small stuff. She lives with her husband, dogs and horses outside of Washington, DC. For more information on her consulting and coaching services, see www.jaeger2.com.

22093763R00076

Made in the USA
Middletown, DE
20 July 2015